The Five Vows

Raising Your Spiritual Commitment to the Next Level

Michael Maciel

Published by FastPencil

Published by FastPencil
307 Orchard City Drive
Suite 210
Campbell CA 95008 USA
info@fastpencil.com
(408) 540-7571
(408) 540-7572 (Fax)
http://www.fastpencil.com

For Calvin

Acknowledgments

How can I possibly thank everyone who has helped me to complete this book? I suppose I could start with those closest to the project: Jenn Fields for her editing expertise; Paula Gillen for her beautiful cover art; John Plummer and Rosamonde Miller for their glowing endorsements; the readers and subscribers to The Mystical Christ weblog, whose feedback has been invaluable to the fine-tuning of the ideas in this book; and to all of my Facebook friends for being such great sounding boards and, at times, my most astute critics. But most of all, I want to thank Bernadette Maciel, who almost never said anything about this project, except when it was absolutely, positively necessary, and then only after I harassed her shamelessly. Her support is and has always been the solid rock beneath my feet.

CONTENTS

PREFACE

The idea for this book came as a result of a conversation I had with my neighbor Jared, a family man and software engineer in Silicon Valley, who wants to live a spiritual life but is not particularly drawn to any church or religion. He grew up in an Catholic family, so he's familiar with religious orders and knows that the members of such communities take vows, and he has a general idea of what those vows are. But like so many others, Jared thinks that vows are for "those" people—nuns, brothers, and priests. He had no concept that he himself could take vows, that he could in effect enter into a personal contract with God, one that would not only come with responsibilities but would also have immediate spiritual benefits. He would not have to give up his wife, his family, or his career to take his spiritual aspirations to the next level.

I explained to Jared that vows are a blessing from God, not a set of rules. They are not an addendum to the Ten Commandments, but rather they are streams of consciousness from the Mind of God into which we enter, sort of like continuous downloads from a server in heaven (I had to speak Jared's language to some extent!)— a stream of consciousness filled with information and updates that would help him adapt to the ever-changing demands of his busy life. At the same time, they would keep him focused in his pursuit of a greater realization of spiritual truth.

The best part for Jared was that no one would be telling him how to run his life. His entire journey in this life would be under his control. The decisions that his life would present to him throughout the coming years would be his and his alone. At no time would another human being, no matter how wise or persuasive, make his decisions for him. This way, I assured him, his own conscience would be the sole authority in his life. His own conscience would be, by virtue

of the vows he could take, a direct link to the
source of universal truth and wisdom.

To Jared, taking vows began to look like a way
to live a spiritual life in this secular world, pri-
vately and autonomously. No one would have to
know of his decision, and no one would be dic-
tating to him how he should live up to those vows
or how he should interpret them. God would do
that, through Jared's own conscience and moral
sense. Jared already knows that what he does
with his life is his responsibility and no one else's.
Taking vows would give his spiritual life structure
and direction.

His autonomy would in no way prevent Jared
from seeking the advice of a spiritual counsellor.
His vows would, however, continually remind
him that whatever course of action he took,
whether by his own reckoning or by the advice of
a teacher, that he would be solely responsible for
it. He would be assuming a level of spiritual
maturity that many seekers never achieve—spiritual self-responsibility.

This book is for you, because chances are that
you have been led to it by a desire similar to
Jared's—to lead a spiritual life without separating

yourself from the things that are important to you. After all, life is to be lived, not merely endured. Life is an opportunity to explore your potential, not a test to see if you can simply follow a set of rules. You have probably already mastered the rules anyway; at least your conscience is developed enough to tell you right from wrong. Now it's time to advance to the next stage of your spiritual journey, to make a meaningful commitment to God, without having to join an order or some other kind of spiritual group. It is possible to live up to your secular responsibilities and also lead a deeply profound and personal spiritual life.

Here is the main idea of this book: *vows are empowering*; they are not restrictive. Vows are designed to align you with Divine consciousness, not separate you from your humanity. The vows facilitate the integration of your human nature with your divine nature; they do not purge or eliminate your earthly identity. The vows recognize that in order to lead a spiritual life *and* be engaged in the world, you must be a fully empowered human being with your head in heaven and your feet on the ground.

This book focuses on the five traditional vows of humility, poverty, service, purity, and obedience. Certainly there are others, but these five form the core, the universal guideposts of the spiritual path.

Just as pride is the greatest sin, humility is the greatest virtue. This book looks primarily at humility, the quality of receptivity. The other vows are subsets of this one over-arching principle. Poverty is the principle of non-attachment as it applies to our possessions—those of the body, the mind, and the spirit. It is the state of consciousness that makes generosity possible. Service has to do with the polarity of our heart and our willingness to give to others without thought of self—that which makes love possible. Purity speaks to our clarity of vision and our ability to focus on the real. Obedience is our willingness to hear the truth as it expresses itself from the core of our being and to follow its dictates, even when everyone else says we are wrong. It is that which enables us to be true to our highest calling.

These four subsets of the vow of humility have one thing in common: they all look to that which is larger than ourselves—God. This is the essence of the spiritual path, the devotion to That which is greater than us. And just as the spiritual path is the road that leads us to God, it is also the road by which God pours grace into the world. The vows are the primary tools of those who have dedicated themselves to this two-way street, this Jacob's Ladder, those whose calling is to act as mediators between heaven and earth, whose dedication to serving humanity supersedes all desire for personal gain.

Here's to you, my fellow servants of the Way.

INTRODUCTION

Vows are principles. They are the generic standards by which we can ensure a healthy and vibrant spiritual life, as universally applicable to our soul as the simple laws of right diet, exercise, and proper rest are for maintaining a healthy body. And just as these simple laws of health are universally applicable to everyone—regardless of race or locale—so are the vows universally applicable, regardless of one's religious calling or spiritual path.

There is one basic spiritual truth: we did not make ourselves. God created us. Even if we do not believe in a "God," the fact remains that we find ourselves in a system that was here before we showed up. Our body, the planet Earth, nature, this solar system—we were born into these with little or no say about them. In an oblique way, we could say that this is the Will of God that theologians talk about. But rather than an individualized prescription, the Divine Will is simply the pattern of creation within which we are born and live out our lives. We did not create the pattern, but when we understand how it works, we can more easily adapt to it and even use it for our benefit.

There are rules—principles of nature—by which we must abide. But as binding as these laws are, they also give us great freedom to explore the potential of what we have been given. Just as the discipline of science has liberated us from ignorance and enabled us to do things that were once deemed impossible, so do the vows—the principles of the science of Spirit—empower us to live a more effective spiritual life.

The keyword in any spiritual discipline is *growth*. This is why we are here. Every soul has a beacon that guides it through the dark night of materiality. To most, that beacon is nameless, though it is usually given the amorphous title "God." The more aware we are of our soul's beacon, the better able we are to integrate our ideas of spirituality into our daily life. It is only by setting a course and sticking to it, overcoming obstacles as they arise and taking advantage of new strengths as they develop, that we are able to grow spiritually.

Unfortunately, vows have been linked with one's commitment to an organized religion or church, which has made them nearly useless in describing the spiritual principles they represent. Ostensibly, vows are taken to God, but *everyone knows* that it's the organization that judges whether they are being kept. This turns vows into a set of rules one must follow. In a world already overburdened by rules, it is no wonder that vows are looked upon with suspicion, even by the most spiritually oriented people.

Vows are intrinsic to spiritual life. They are its basic framework. They are broad enough in scope that we can apply them to any religious practice, and yet they are scientific enough that we can apply them to any mundane activity as well. As principles, the vows are as useful to us in our programs of spiritual development as the laws of thermodynamics are to engineering.

Since vows are *principles*, spiritual aspirants hold them in deep contemplation until they become amalgamated with their soul. The key to this amalgamation is action. As we live the principles, we rewire our thinking. Every time we choose to act in accordance with our vows instead of catering to old habits, we become more receptive to God's influence in our lives. This is the process of atonement, or *at-one-ment* —the attunement of our human nature with the Divine.

Through right action, we align ourselves with God. But, what is *right action*? This is a little like asking what is spiritual. The tendency is to think that right action and spirituality are objective forms of behavior, sets of rules that we can follow, conduct we can measure according to recognized standards. In reality, while they are universally real and applicable to all, right action and spirituality always express themselves uniquely in the lives of individuals. The principle is universal; the expression is unique. As long as we remain focused on the principle, our actions will eventually come into alignment, naturally and organically. But the principle must exist for us as a possibility, not as a fixed idea, not as a definition of right action, or a clear-cut image of what it's like to be spiritual. We have to hold in mind the understanding that we *do not know* what the principles are, not in their complete reality, and yet remain open to the Divine influence they make possible. Our conception of these principles will grow as we grow.

By taking vows, we create a line of demarcation in the span of our life, establishing a point of departure from the world mind. When we ritualize the event, we formalize it. We make it a definitive action in the presence of our spiritual community and in the presence of God. Witnesses add their spiritual support; they *bless* our new level of life. And since the vows themselves are blessings from the Divine, the entire action is a positive flow of spiritual energies. The language of the vows, along with our understanding and acceptance of them, creates the patterns into which we will live our lives. These patterns give our spiritual life focus and direction, thus empowering us to achieve the transformation we seek.

1

THE UNNAMED CALLING

There's nothing like an unnamed calling to keep you up at night. You know you should be doing something more with your life but you don't know what. You might have the feeling that your passion—art, the environment, children, politics, whatever—is on the verge of a breakthrough, as though some new thing were welling up from the depths, a spiritual realization that has yet to breach the surface of your awareness. It feels like a looming presence whose stare is fixed on you, a presence that can be felt but not seen.

Such an impending emergence in our lives can feel ominous if we let it. Someone unaccustomed to spiritual presences might find it so. But for those who are mystically inclined, what looms just out of sight feels more like something wanting to be born, something undeniably important.

The excitement of the new emergence can be maddening. It can feel like there's a barrier keeping the new realization coming out, as though something is sitting on it, preventing it from seeing the light of day. Intuitively, you suspect that it's *you* who's getting in the way, that whatever it is that's trying to make itself known is waiting for you to step aside, to relax your expectations, to relinquish some false belief or idea about what it is you should be doing with your life. It's as though the new thing wants assurance that your rational mind won't rip it apart the moment it exposes itself, trying to force-fit it into ideas you already have, instead of letting it show you something truly new.

So, you resort to any and all methods you can think of to get at it, to help the bubble burst and allow the new thing to breathe. Meditation becomes important to you; you begin to probe the very depths from which the new thing is trying to free itself. But unless you can leave your preconceptions and expectations behind, your presence there can look like a threat, and the thing you're seeking recedes farther into the darkness.

It is then that you realize that you have to start dismantling those preconceptions and expectations, to let go of them and assume the inner posture of being willing to accept the new thing as it is and not try to remake it into something familiar the moment it comes into view. You begin to realize that you might have to coax it from behind the amniotic curtain that separates it from your conscious awareness. Instead of midwife, you become the courtier, wooing the unknown out of its shyness and into your arms. You lay down your preconceptions and expectations and invite it to be what it is, with the promise that you will not impose your everyday biases upon it. Instead of grabbing for it, you let it come to you in its own time.

In order to coax the emerging realization into your waking consciousness, soliciting its physical expression into your life, you must undergo a certain amount of preparation. One cannot put something new into something old. You cannot expect a higher vibration to blend seamlessly with a lower vibration, lest the discordancy shake the whole thing apart. So you begin with certain inner disciplines. You examine your pride—the exaggerated sense of self-worth that inclines you to believe that anything new that comes from within will automatically match what you already know. You make the conscious effort to acknowledge that the sheer tonnage of what you don't know vastly outweighs your current understanding of both the cosmos and your place in it. You start to listen more carefully to other people, giving them the benefit of the doubt, entertaining the notion that they might have something of value to offer you, even those whom you would normally regard as being less enlightened. You make yourself available to wisdom no matter what outlet it chooses to make itself known, knowing that as you do so, you pave the way for the true wisdom, the Noble Sophia, whom you so badly want to know, to come forth into your waiting embrace.

The quality of spirit you must cultivate for this to happen is humility. Humility is the entrance fee to the spiritual path, the prerequisite to experiencing the reality of God. And rather than the self-effacing, grovelling sense of worthlessness that the ego finds so frightening, humility is just the opposite. It is the burgeoning awareness that reality is *so large!* It's not that we are so small, it's that God is so big. We don't have to artificially construct an obsequious attitude, we just allow ourselves to be blown away by the magnificence of it all. Any inflated sense we have of our own significance is automatically rendered irrelevant.

As a spiritual quality, humility is not acquired through study alone. It must be recognized as a state of consciousness that one must enter into. Humility is an aspect of God's personality, which might seem contradictory to the notion of what it means to be humble (How could God be humble?). But as illogical as this may sound, it is only our human sense of logic that finds it so. Like the hammer that sees everything as a nail, the ego sees everything as a mirror. Since the ego thinks that it's a god worthy of all worship, the idea that God is also humble seems…well, ungodlike.

It's helpful to think of God's personality as being like the sun. Its aspects stream forth as beams of light that vivify everything they land upon. They have a kind of wave form, a distinct frequency that leaves footprints on our soul. Our thoughts about humility activate these footprints, and we sense them as evidence that something living has left a path for us to follow. The Sanskrit word *marga* means the path left by an animal. It means more, however, than the marks in the dirt or the pheromones in the air. *Marga* alludes to this kind of trail, but insinuates a trail of a higher vibratory nature. When an advanced soul, such as Jesus or Buddha, lives out his life of service on Earth, he leaves a "trail"—his ideas, his choices, and the connections that make up his experience of the Divine. The quality of these aspects, their *scent*, if you will, is a feeling with which we can easily resonate. That feeling is *awe*.

Awe is not an aspect we normally associate with people such as Jesus or Buddha. We tend to think of them as deities, their soul-personalities raining down upon us in a strictly top-down, hierarchical way. But, it is precisely their *awe* that makes them mediators. If we look to them as the pinnacle of Spirit, we commit the very sin that they warned against. Buddha said, "The finger pointing at the moon is not the moon," referring to himself as the teacher, not the goal. And Jesus said, "I am the way;" never did he say, "I am God." When we connect with Jesus' feeling of awe, the feeling he has when he "lifts his eyes to heaven," the vibratory signature of that feeling magnetizes our inner compass and establishes our true north forever.

The scent of the aspect of God's personality that we detect has a bit of God in it, the "hem of the garment," so to speak. So, when we come in contact with it, we are coming in contact with God. The vibratory pattern we are picking up matches exactly the vibratory pattern of the aspect. In other words, the scent is *alive*. It is not a remnant or an artifact; it's a direct connection with the thing itself. Once we touch it, or are touched by it, we will never be able to let it go.

Once the aspect is activated on a person's soul, it remains there as a living presence, continually pointing the way to its source. It becomes part of our soul's makeup. We can ignore it, but it is always there. We will never feel complete within ourselves until we acknowledge its presence and submit to its calling. When we finally surrender to it, its vibration permeates our entire being. We are changed from the inside out. No one needs to tell us "lo here! or, lo there!" because we *know* where the path is. It is within us.

Over the centuries, those who have trod this inner path have found ways to help new travellers by putting them in direct touch with this aspect of God's personality—humility—which makes possible the sense of awe, forever giving them an inner path to follow. The mechanism by which this is done is the vow. Unfortunately, taking vows has become, in our scientific age, merely a public ceremony, an outward expression of one's intention to live up to one's word—a promise. And while there's nothing wrong with that, this interpretation falls far short of reality. We need a new interpretation, a new way to understand what it means to take vows.

RE-ENVISIONING THE VOWS

The last thing most people want to do is to vow themselves to something—an organization, a religion, a spiritual teacher. Rightfully so. There are too many examples of the abuse of power per-petrated in the name of spirituality. Even when vows are administered with the understanding that they are taken to God and not to an organi-zation or a person, they usually wind up becoming just that—a means to govern and con-trol the spiritual lives of others. The entire con-cept of vows needs to be re-envisioned in a way that serves people, not corral them into a pre-scribed ideology or way of living.

The vows are not about what we have to do, nor are they about what we have to *not* do. The vows are states of divine consciousness. Taking them opens the door to the experience of those states. Thinking that you will have to change yourself if you take vows is like thinking that you will have to change your personality if you move to a different city. You will take on a different character with time, that's for sure, but that isn't something you can make happen. No one changes by force of will, either ours or someone else's. God does the changing. All we have to do is show up.

Basic moral principles are designed to bring the animal part of our nature up to a certain level of refinement and development. We learn these principles as we live our lives. But the tendency is to think that we have to continually revisit them, because the slightest act of selfishness, pride, avarice, anger, or lust can cause us to feel guilt. We start to doubt ourselves, and we begin to feel unworthy of the Higher Mysteries of Illumination, Self-realization, and the Priesthood. If we try to perfect that which has already been sufficiently established, we are only wasting valuable time. Besides, it's egotistical to strive for perfection, because perfection serves no purpose in this world, except to prove ourselves better than others. In order to be effective in our spiritual life, we have to embrace the idea that *good is good enough.*

Learning basic moral principles also raises our consciousness to the level where we can recognize the existence of higher worlds. The farther we progress on the spiritual path, the less important physical survival becomes. Maslow's Hierarchy of Needs, as Joseph Campbell points out, carries no weight in the lives of artists and mystics. One's *vision* is the important thing, even more important than life itself (*"He who loses his life will find it*"). We all have a vision; it's what carries us forward in our spiritual strivings. If we are not obedient to the energies that arise out of that vision, our life becomes a living hell.

We should not try to turn the vows into enforcement mechanisms, as many have tried to do in the past. The laws of God have been written in our hearts, and no one needs to tell us right from wrong. Usually, disobeying our conscience requires a concerted effort on our part, whereas in the earlier stages of our spiritual evolution we had no choice but to simply obey our instincts. Our conscience was not yet fully formed.

The vows are openings into higher states of consciousness. They are meant for us to use as tools to help us achieve our higher calling into God-consciousness. They are made *for us*—we are not made for them. We know that we are on the spiritual path; no one has to coax us. No one has to convince us that we should seek reality. We already know that that's what we want, and we look for anything and everything that will help us get there. If we can see the vows as aids along the Way, they start to look attractive. We take them willingly. We understand that they strengthen our relationship with God, not weaken it. We don't need layers of intermediaries between us and the Self. Rather than tell us what we have to do, the vows *immerse* us in the spiritual energies they represent. We come into the higher levels of consciousness at a natural pace, which allows for deeper and therefore longer-lasting integration with our personality. We *become* the virtues, not just adopt them.

VOWS—WHY TAKE THEM?

In the final scene of the 1991 movie *Grand Canyon*, the characters drive to the Grand Canyon and see it for the first time. The entire movie up until this point has been about the chaos in their lives, their dramas and traumas and self-absorption, all of which are of epic proportion. But when they get out of the car and see the immensity of the landscape in front of them, all of their problems are obliterated in that moment. If you've ever been to the Grand Canyon, you know what I mean. Being in its presence can literally take your breath away.

Spiritual experiences are like seeing the Grand Canyon for the first time. They have the power to transform your life. When you experience the presence of God for the first time, your life is changed forever. The power is overwhelming. Technically, the word "power" means the capacity to do work—the ability to change things. Spiritual power is the sense we get of being in the presence of an infinite potential, a living energy that both knows and hears us, an energy that is at once both vast and intimately close. It makes us feel incredibly small and at the same time enormously important—*"So small between the stars, so large against the sky,"* as Leonard Cohen so artfully puts it—a presence so powerful that we can feel ourselves instantly lifted into a different reality. This is real power, the kind we all seek when we embark upon the spiritual path.

Sometimes, we can sense this kind of power around another person, usually a spiritual teacher, but not always. We get the sense that the power they are exuding is coming *through* them, not from them. They are the channel for it, not its source. This is a wonderful experience, and we're fortunate to come into contact with him or her. Jesus was such a person. So was Buddha, and so many others, both living and dead.

There is power in taking vows. It may not seem like it, given that so many vow rituals are treated as though they don't really matter, as though they were merely a formality, or something nice to do. Or they might be thought of as simply a promise one makes to God, as though the person taking the vow is the giver and God the receiver. This would be like trying to stuff electricity into a wall socket—clearly a misunderstanding of the principles involved.

Another common misconception of vows is that they derive their power from consensus. By stating our intention in front of witnesses, they somehow strengthen our resolve. But this too misses the reality. The power to perform does not come from taking vows, nor does it come from our desire to live up to our word. Power is there, but it doesn't come from us, and it doesn't come from another person. However, it can come through another person, if they know themselves to be a channel for it and can get out of the way, letting the grace of God do its work.

Vows are more than just concepts; they are a living part of the Mind of God. Being alive, they act upon those who enter into them. Being part of the Mind of God, their action never ceases. The action of each vow is different from the others. If we can understand the action, we can understand what the action does. The important thing to understand is that it is not we who are doing the action, but God. We let the vows act upon us.

Action is perhaps the most important distinction to make when it comes to understanding God and Spirit. Action is power manifesting as energy. This energy moves from a source, through a medium, to a receiver. The application of energy upon a receiver is called *force*. So, you have three elements: power, energy, and force. Force, scientifically speaking, is neutral. A rolling ball striking a wall exerts a force upon the wall; it is not "forcing" the wall to do something the wall doesn't want to do. This isn't a metaphor, an obscuration of scientific meaning. Force, in the context in which we are speaking, means *energy applied*, nothing more.

Along with action, there is another word cru-
cial to understanding vows. Some might call it
"reality," but that word, like "love," has many different meanings. When someone says, "I love
you," it has a different meaning from when they
say, "I *luv* you." When something is *real*, we mean
that it is a part of God—an aspect of the Divine
that   is   all-pervasive,   all-inclusive,   and
eternal. *Reality*, for the sake of this discussion,
does not mean my reality or your reality; it
means that which is real to God. Of course, we
cannot know completely what God's reality is,
but we can assume that it exists. Our act of
assumption at least makes more of it available to
us and gives us new and useful ways to understand it.

For instance, things that are real to God appear
archetypal to us—over-arching, abstract, non-
specific. Like love. The word "love" is a general
term to us, but for God it is highly specific. Love
is either present or it is not. Love is a part of
God's being, an aspect of God's personality
woven into the fabric of reality. It is not a concept. So, if we know this about love, and we have
experienced it, we can enter into the reality of

love as though we were entering into an energy field, one that is alive and sentient. Since love is an essential aspect of God, when we experience the reality of love, we are experiencing the reality of God.

Remember the three-part principle of power, energy, and force? Well, if a person has gotten in touch with the reality of love, then that person becomes a channel of love for other people. Through the connection we all have with each other, the real displaces the unreal—the energy moves from an area of higher concentration to an area of lower concentration. And if a person is receptive to this flow of energy, a force will be applied and a transformation will take place.

TRANSFORMATION

Transformation is the purpose of taking vows. Otherwise, why take them? But like the words "love" and "reality," transformation has been transformed into something different from its spiritual meaning. Transformation is usually thought of as changing into something new, whereas in its spiritual context it means changing *back* to the way God originally created us. It washes clean the encrusted self in order to reveal that which was there all the time, only hidden. It is the *return* to our own Divine Nature.

When a person of high consciousness acts as a channel for God to immerse a willing person in the real energy of God's own being, the person receiving the blessing is cleansed of the false energy patterns created by years of illusionary thinking and behaving. A vow is a blessing. It is a movement of divine energy that bestows grace upon the receiver, enabling him or her to overcome the inertia of the sensory world. Vows enliven the divine spark within us.

Let's explore, now, the Five Vows.

2

HUMILITY—A QUALITY OF BEING

You may have heard the story of the prospective student and the overflowing teacup. The master pours his visitor a cup of tea and then keeps pouring even as the tea starts spilling out onto the floor. The prospective student is alarmed and offended. He questions whether the master knows what he is doing, whereupon the master informs him that just as there is no room in his cup for more tea, there is no more room in his mind for further teaching. The student thinks he already knows what the master is going to say and is therefore non-receptive.

Humility is all about being receptive. It is the willingness and the ability to learn. It is the foundation of successful spiritual training. And it does not come by degree—you are either humble or you are not. You may cycle in and out of the state of being humble, but there is no such thing as partial humility.

It has been said that the ego is the first thing to be attracted to the spiritual path and the last thing to let go. It takes one look at the possibility of spiritual development and says, "Hey, this is for me! I can really *use* this to make myself look important." When spirituality becomes a system of knowledge rather than a quality of being, it's just one more merit badge on the ego's uniform. High achievers will naturally be drawn to the spiritual path, because it has a reputation for being difficult. This isn't such a bad thing, because it is difficult, and it can take a considerable amount of self-confidence to weather the disappointments that the ego will have to endure before it gives up willingly.

Therefore, you will probably be learning humility your entire life. The moment you think that you have it is the exact moment you do not.

And this will never cease to be an issue, not as long as you are living on Earth in a physical body. This is why that in all valid courses of spiritual study, humility comes first—not high-minded theories, or tidbits of information designed to impress you, or that you can use to impress others.

NOT-KNOWING

The state of not-knowing is a source of great power. Humility is a virtue, but in order for virtues to be spiritually useful, they must be empowering. They must open a way in us to manifest the life and power of the Spirit. Not-knowing gives us a way to create that opening.

For example, the scientist who admits to herself that she's not seeing the whole picture is in a much more powerful position than she who thinks she knows what she's looking at. (All the best scientists are humble.) In this case, the power lies in being open to something new, no matter how much it might fly in the face of what one already knows. The same applies to our spiritual searching. For are we not scientists also, seeking to know what is real?

It's one thing to say, "I don't know." It's quite another to put yourself into a state of not-knowing so that the real can show up. To say "I don't know" only amounts to a negative, self-limiting prayer if it fails to take that stance as a means of pulling the truth out of the Cosmic Mind. What good does it do to be humble if it only keeps us ignorant?

Saying "I don't know" may be appropriate for a novice, because it puts one in a receptive frame of mind. It makes us teachable. But the mature Christian mystic seeks his or her wisdom from within. Here is where humility becomes a tool, not as a means to boost one's ego, but to raise one's consciousness to a higher level. *Nature abhors a vacuum.* Not-knowing turns the mind into a vacuum, a vacuum that must be filled.

"Not this, not that," says the Upanishads. When the mind jumps in with an answer, the wise meditator says, "Not this, not that." The mind then says, "Well, how about this?" to which the wise meditator says, "Not that either." Eventually, through the process of elimination, the field of mind is cleared and the truth comes bursting in.

The truth cannot be destroyed. We slay our concepts until none are left standing. That which remains is devoid of our concepts. It may not be the *ultimate* truth, but it will always be closer to it than anything we have seen before.

When a person of high consciousness, one who also has the authority to administer vows, gets in touch with the reality of humility and then escorts another into that same state of consciousness—one who has stated his or her intention to experience it—then the Holy Spirit moves, and the vow is placed upon that person's soul, not as a burden, but as a blessing, a pattern of power that will assist that person in his or her journey toward God-realization.

God's consciousness flows into the world like water into a garden. The energy of Spirit is raw and undifferentiated. It cares not who is just or unjust, but rather gives to all alike. It nurtures souls according to their need, bringing to fruition their deepest, most fervent desires. To be humble is to get out of the way of the process and let it work. God knows what to do. People who have attained to the consciousness of humility live in a state of constant wonder and amazement at the miracles taking place all around them.

Try this: Pick any ordinary object, such as an apple. Look at it for a full minute, then ask your mind, "Is this an apple?" The mind will say, "What, are you kidding? Of course it's an apple!" But being rule-bound as all minds are, it has to take your question seriously. So it digs deeper. It begins to throw out all of the assumptions and categories into which apples have been placed and seeks a wider and deeper context in which to interpret the object called "apple." All of a sudden, the apple no longer looks like *just an apple* .

If you do this exercise right, you will be amazed at what you haven't been seeing. The mind likes to think in words. When you challenge those words, it forces the mind to reconsider, to re-examine the thing it has been taking for granted. After using this technique on common, ordinary objects, you might want to turn it on yourself. Look in the mirror and ask, "Am I a human being?" This will open some doors, believe me. Depending on your stamina, you will see things about human being that may surprise you. And if you're humble, you won't take it personally.

THE TEMPTATION IN THE WILDERNESS

When Jesus was preparing to go public with his mission, he encountered three negative aspects within himself that first had to be expunged.

First, there was the desire to fulfill his physical appetites: "Turn these stones into bread." Next came fear: "Throw yourself off of this cliff." And finally (saving the best for last) came pride, and I will paraphrase: "You have the power to fix all the problems of the world, so who could be better for the task? It is your *duty*, therefore, to take charge, to tell people what to do."

The first step in spiritual development is learning how *not* to impose our will on others. We teach by providing opportunities for others to grow. Growth is why we are all here, so there is no need to inculcate this desire in another person. Growth is the soul's primary motivation, leading us into every experience we encounter.

So, let your motivation be one of service, and never place an obstacle in the path of another's journey toward the realization of God. Do not take away their opportunity to grow by making their decisions for them.

The prime directive for spiritually-minded people is the same as it is for physicians: "Do No Harm."

BLESSED ARE THE POOR IN SPIRIT

The directness of Jesus' words in The Sermon on the Mount tells us that he is addressing those who are sincerely seeking wisdom and not those who are merely looking for something to think about. The audience is not the general public but rather a group of applicants for discipleship. So what he has to say deals more with the necessary character traits one must have in order to qualify for discipleship, not points of philosophy. And the very first trait—you guessed it—is humility.

These people are God-seekers. They are not asking for rules to follow, but rather they want to know how they should *be*—more precisely, what their attitude of being should be in order to achieve enlightenment. They are looking for "be-attitudes." So, Jesus gives them the most important attitude of being right up front: "Blessed are the poor in spirit, for theirs is the kingdom of heaven."

As a serious spiritual student, you are looking for more than just knowledge—you are looking for a quality of being. And while knowledge is certainly a part of that, it is not the goal; it is an *aid* for reaching the goal—Christ-consciousness. But while knowledge can help us, it can also be our biggest obstacle to God-realization, because the ideas we possess often define who we are to ourselves. So, Jesus is telling his prospective students that in order to receive the truth from him, they must not be attached to what they already know. They must be *poor* in spirit.

Jesus is also telling them that Christ-consciousness is *higher* consciousness, that the truth of God is not necessarily going to fit in with their pre-existing concepts. We like things to be consistent with what we already know. So, he warns them not to listen solely for those ideas that will reinforce the opinions they already have. They have to be willing to let go of their ideas and be receptive to new ones. He is telling them that they are going to have to be humble.

On the spiritual path, we seek that which is greater than ourselves. But the lesser cannot comprehend the greater—thus the importance of humility. Unless we can empty our mind of all preconceptions and adopt what Buddhists call "beginner's mind," we cannot receive anything more than what we already know. There will be no room in the inn.

All Streams flow to the sea
because it is lower than they are.
Humility gives it its power.
—Lao-tzu

TRUST

Humility is impossible without trust. You have to know that God intends you no harm but only wants your absolute good. This is fundamental to your spiritual growth. Otherwise, you will always be protective and not receptive, and you will subordinate your intuitions to your rational mind for its approval, a task for which it is entirely unsuited.

Trust is the real message within the saying, "God loves you." God is not vindictive or prejudiced or given to favoritism. God does not punish or condemn anyone for any reason. These are concepts invented by theologians to keep people afraid. If you are afraid of God, you will not be able to open up to the subtle energies that will come to you during meditation—the energies that will transform you.

Humility, trust, meditation—this is the format.

GETTING REAL

Unless humility can be explained in terms of power, energy, and force, it can be of little use to us in our quest for Self-realization. We have to find out what humility is *really*. If it motivates a movement of the Spirit, we need to know how. Spirit is real, it is capable of producing effects in our lives, and it heals people. It is not a theological concept, though many have tried to make it that. We need more. If Spirit is real, we need to know how it works, and humility is the key.

If you can sense the power of God, if you have a sense of life as energy in action and not just a set of circumstances, if you've had the experience of seeing the world pregnant with possibility, bursting from within with the urge to demon-strate itself in outward manifestation, if you know it as the "force that through the green fuse drives the flower," then you know that Spirit is real.

Spirit is not just energy, it is also intelligence. It is sentient, and it pours itself into the world in a way that can only be described as love. Whether we are conscious of it or not, Spirit is always working, always expressing. It does so because it *has* to—moving into form is its very nature. Once we know this about it, our most natural reaction is to want it to move towards us. Once we know that God is real and not just a concept, once we know God and not just believe in God, we want the experience, and we want as much of it as we can get. And when we have it, we want to share it, because sharing it increases its power. The more power it has, the more we can experience it, so we share it as much as possible.

As a word, "humility" has lost nearly all of its meaning, because it does not address the aliveness of God. If we saw God as the source of Life, we would rush toward God with eagerness. But the word "humility," the way it is used today, would have us crawl toward God in shame in a kind of reverse egotism that would deny the flow of life energy that is God's will to bestow upon us.

The Spirit cleans everything it touches, so why feel shame? Shame and humility are antithetical to each other. Shame is a clever dodge by the ego to keep itself in play. In order to be truly humble, shame has to go.

Humility is the *expectation* of a movement of the Spirit. It doesn't try to force that movement —it knows the movement will happen. It knows the same way a catcher knows that the ball is going to land in his glove. He doesn't even have to think it, because he *IS* it. The way you can tell if a person is truly humble is by the way he *expects* God to act. Certainty of fulfillment is the hall-mark of humility.

How does this work? How can we be certain that God will act in accordance with our expecta-tions? Is it realistic to think that God will come through in the way we expect? If we were dealing with another human being, then we would have no right to expect anything from them with any degree of certainty—unless, of course, it's a motorcycle cop. If you speed past a motorcycle cop who has his radar gun homed in on you, the chances of him NOT pursuing you are about as good as winning the lottery. Why? Because the motorcycle cop HAS to chase you if you are speeding. It's the law. In the same way, God HAS to respond to our expectations, if those expectations are based in reality.

We have to think of God as the functional fabric of reality. Our thoughts continually pour into the Mind of God. If our thoughts are consistent with the laws of nature, and we do not weaken our thoughts with contradictory thinking, then we can reasonably expect that our physical reality will mirror the ideas we picture in the Mind of God.

Everywhere we see people who feel defeated in life because they believe that God doesn't particularly like them. They feel shame about things they've done, or they buy into what others have told them about how you have to be "lucky" to do well in life. They think of God as a father figure, one who is too much like their own father, the one who never gave them a break. This way of thinking about God is anthropomorphic in the worst possible way. It's the kind of thinking that we must rid ourselves of completely. Why?

Because it simply is not in accordance with reality.

We don't have to be religious to accept the notion of the Mind of God. In fact, it helps if we throw out our religious sentiments altogether, at least for a moment, so that we can think about God scientifically. Here's what I mean: matter is composed of patterns of intelligence. The molecular and atomic structure of matter is nothing more than vibrating energy, and it vibrates in very specific ways, each element according to its place on the Periodic Table of the Elements. And not only does it vibrate, it is continually changing its vibrations every time it interacts with another bit of matter. These interactions are, in a sense, relationships, and like any relationship, they change as circumstances change. We are, in the most real sense, living in a sea of interacting, energetic relationships, each of which MUST behave according to the laws of physics.

Just because we say that matter is composed of patterns of intelligence doesn't mean that it is self-conscious. The intelligence of matter is automatic, the same way that most of our bodily functions are automatic. If we think of the physical universe as the "body" of God, then it's easy to see that, like our body, much of what happens in our physical reality happens automatically. Just as our physical body responds to the tone of our thoughts—our habitual ways of thinking and the feelings we pump into them—the world at large responds to the thinking that we humans think into it.

You can either accept this proposition or reject it, but it's worth your serious consideration. And unlike other, more philosophical propositions, this one you can test. If you have sufficient control of your thoughts and emotions and are capable of filling your mental atmosphere with the visions and feelings that you want to experience, then you will see that this works. Do it often enough, and you will expect it to work every time you activate it. You will expect it with such certainty that you would be shocked if it didn't happen. You would expect it the same way you expect the light to come on when you flip the light switch. You would expect it the same way you expect your letter to reach its destination when you drop it in the mailbox. You don't expect it because you think you're special; you expect it because that's how things work. Do this, and that happens. Simple cause and effect.

When the centurion asked Jesus in the eighth chapter of Matthew to heal his servant, he didn't expect him to actually come to his house and do it personally. That would have been like expecting the mailman to personally deliver the letter we dropped in the mailbox. The centurion knew how power, energy, and force works: "Just say the word, and my servant will be healed. For I myself am a man under authority, with soldiers under me. I tell this one, 'Go,' and he goes; and that one, 'Come,' and he comes. I say to my servant, 'Do this,' and he does it." Jesus was impressed. He could see that the centurion understood the laws of creation better than his own students. Space and time can offer no resistance to the word of one who is truly humble.

What the scientific community today doesn't accept is that mind has anything to do with physical reality. They concede that stress affects our health, but they don't believe that our stress affects someone else's health. Parents who are at all perceptive know that there is a bond between them and their kids. What the parent thinks, the child feels. That's easy enough to see, but it helps to understand that our thoughts and feelings are not restricted to the confines of our skull. We are broadcasting stations, and like the patterns of intelligence that make up the physical world of atoms and molecules, our thoughts and feelings make up the world of our experience. What we put out we get back. The tenor of our thoughts creates the relationships we have with the world. We get what we expect. There are times when it doesn't work out the way we want it to, but this is just the inertia of the world. If we persist and we work in accordance with mental law, the conditions we want will assert themselves in our lives more and more until they are the predominant pattern.

When we are truly humble, we expect things to work. We expect them to work because we know that they don't need us in order to do what they are supposed to do. The light switch connects the power generated at the power plant to the light bulb; we don't magically cause the electricity to flow. It's not *our* power. We tell it what to do, we don't force it with our superior intelligence and will. Just imagine what it would be like if every time we went to turn on the lights we had to do an internal inventory to see if we were worthy enough to cause the electricity to flow. We might feel like we had to meditate first, or maybe help an elderly person take out their garbage, or say a rosary. Each time we went to flip the switch, we'd say to ourselves, "God, I hope this is gonna work!"

"God makes the rain to fall on the just and the unjust alike." The reason that good things sometimes happen to bad people is that bad people are usually good at knowing what they want and have a ruthless determination to get it. They don't care if other people get hurt in the process. I'm not condoning that kind of behavior. I'm simply pointing out that there is a way that things work, and until we really get that, we cannot use power effectively. As long as we believe that we are the source of power, we will never be able to summon enough of it to make a difference. We cannot by force of will "make one hair white or black." But when we know that power is all around us and that it is perfectly willing and able to respond to our intentions, then we can use it to make our lives and the lives of others better.

One more thing about humility and power:
when we find ourselves caught up in a situation
where other people are using power in a way
that's interfering with our happiness, we learn
right away that any resistance on our part only
makes the situation worse. Why? Because we are
caught in the belief that we have to overpower
the energies in play. This never works, and if it
does seem to work, it only works temporarily.
Energy can be steered, but it cannot be
destroyed. Once in motion, we have to deal with
it on its own terms. We have to redirect it, not tell
it to stop. Energy does not know "stop." It only
knows that it has to play itself out in a way that is
consistent with its momentum. When we know
that, life gets a lot easier. You don't try to stop a
punch with your face; you step aside and let the
unconnected swing throw your assailant off balance. Then, *you* are in control of the situation.

GOD'S HUMILITY

One way we can tell that our normal understanding of humility is insufficient is by entertaining the idea that God is also humble, that
humility is not just a human virtue but a divine
principle. Humility is a necessary component of

creative power. Without humility there can be no power and no creativity. Humility is the source of power. Humility is the vacuum that nature abhors.

While it is true that God can create anything, God still has to abide by God's own laws, not because God is restricted but because Law—*principle*—is part of God's nature. God can create in no other way. When Genesis says that we were created in God's image and likeness, this means that we too are bound by the laws of creation. We cannot simply wish things into being. There is a *way* in which creation takes place, and in order to get in touch with the vast empty space of divine undifferentiated potential, we have to empty ourselves of the belief in limitation. This requires great humility.

Let's examine the statement "God knows everything." This idea is meaningless and therefore misleading. The rules for creativity are the same for God as they are for us—we have to know nothing before we can know anything. Divine, undifferentiated potential is *no*-thing. It is empty and void and yet pregnant with the ability to *become*. In the beginning, according to

Genesis, "Darkness was upon the face of the deep." The vast, undifferentiated potential of God's own being is where God had to start in the creative process. It is into that potentiality that God spoke the Word, and the worlds were brought into being.

Not-knowing creates a space within which all things are possible. Not-knowing breaks down the barriers that keep us imprisoned in the known. The known is a parched desert, what Jean Baudrillard called "the desert of the real"— nothing grows there. Once a thing is known, it ceases to live. Not-knowing is the key to life. You can't exist in a state of not-knowing and believe that God knows everything. If God knew everything, everything would cease to be. It is God's not-knowing that keeps the universe growing and evolving. It is the very thing that generates life.

Consider that our greatest awakening occurs in the space created by not-knowing. Why would it be different for God? We are the microcosm of the macrocosm. What is true for us is true for It. If we believe in statements like "Man, know thyself" and "We are created in God's image and likeness," then we have to afford God that which provides the opening within us—not-knowing.

Only in a society caught in the glamour of the intellect, a society that values knowledge and information above all else, can you find the concept that God knows everything. When knowing everything is the highest concept of good, then naturally the god of that society must epitomize that concept. But the mystic knows better. The mystic knows that in order for God to be the creator of all life, there must be that within God which creates the emptiness within which life can occur. Unless the universe holds that space within Itself, the whole thing would grind to a halt.

The one thing that is guaranteed to produce movement (life) is a vacuum. When we stand in the place of not-knowing, we effectively create a vacuum in the universal mind, the Mind of God. God then rushes in to fill the vacuum that we make ourselves to be.

In order to understand this concept, we have to think in terms of power, energy, and force. God is not an external entity—God is the living, sentient being in Whom we live. The only thing that keeps us from the experience of God is the belief that we exist as a separate self. This is the lie perpetrated by our own senses. When we turn away from the senses and go into the silence within ourselves, we begin to experience God as a presence. And by that I mean a living power that knows and experiences us to the degree that we know and experience It. God's love is a two-way street—love begets love, although, "we love because He first loved us."

Taking the phrase "first loved us" out of the context of space and time, which is what we have to do if we want to know God, "first loved us" means that we exist in a field of love, a conscious energy that is always here and now. "First loved us" means that *we did not create it* —it was already here when we arrived. But when we get quiet within ourselves and open up to it, we allow love to occur in the world. This is our place in the scheme of things. As Unity teacher Eric Butterworth put it, "We are an inlet and an outlet of God."

It is imperative that we stop thinking of God as something external. God is that which keeps the Cosmos in motion, from the very smallest to the infinitely big. It is all one thing. Emerson said, "There is no great and no small to the mind that maketh all." Size and distance are creations of the mind. They do not exist in God's reality. If we want to know God, we have to be *like* God and think the way God thinks. This is not as difficult as it might sound, because, again, God knows nothing about difficulty, either large or small. We need only ask for help and help is given. And asking is intrinsically humble.

As a side note, when a spiritual teacher pushes the idea that God knows everything, what he's really saying is, "*I* know more than you do." The assumption is that the teacher is closer to God and therefore naturally knows more of what God knows. This is a well-known tactic to gain power over one's students. The true teacher, on the other hand, seeks to draw students into the state of not-knowing, so that together, the entire community can become one with God in that state. The Buddha of Compassion, Avalokitesvara, vowed not to enter into enlightenment until all sentient beings were saved. And in Hebrews 8 we read, "And they shall not teach, each one his neighbor and each one his brother, saying,'Know the Lord,' for they shall all know me, from the least of them to the greatest." Not-knowing is the Causeless Cause of the act of creation. It is the organizing principle of all that is. "Of myself, I do *nothing* ." This is humility.

CONTEMPLATION

Humility is the sign of a spiritually mature person, but it is important that you not forget everything you have learned prior to beginning your training—that would be naive. You have to practice meditation in order to expose yourself to higher consciousness and be changed by it, but unless you integrate what you receive into the "body" of you, what you receive will do you little good. Here we have the true function of the rational mind, but it can only function properly if it is humble.

The rational mind is the *servant* of the Self, not its censor; at least, this is what it should be. The term "bride of Christ" is a metaphor for the relationship of the rational mind to the Self. The proper role of the rational mind is to receive intuitions and to integrate them into our experiences. Part of this function is to test and prove that which is received—not because the intuition might be faulty (it never is), but because what is received might not be entirely clear or complete.

For this, we have contemplation, which we learn to do after we have become proficient in meditation. In contemplation, we let go of the steering wheel of our mind, so to speak, and let our thoughts think themselves. A new thought has a life of its own and will show you things about itself that you could never figure out with your intellect. This differs significantly from simply letting your mind wander in that it takes a mastery of concentration before a thought can stick to its own trajectory without being deflected by an unrelated thought. Meditation is the act of receiving thoughts and impressions from the Higher Mind. It is the mastery of receptivity, requiring a profound stillness in our personal mind and equilibrium in our emotions.

One manifestation of contemplation is inspiration. During meditation, we might receive a melody, one that we want to use in a song we're working on. But the melody we hear is only a fragment, so we can either take the fragment and flesh it out with our intellect, or we can sit with the fragment and let it fill itself in. This is contemplation. It takes a well-trained intellect to allow this to occur. We have to hold our intellect in check so that the Higher Mind can express itself without interference. Our intellect can observe, but we must not let it intervene.

It takes a lot of work to achieve this level of thinking.

Contemplation requires a subtle, unbiased state of mind in which you gently view each new idea as though it were a precious gemstone with many facets. But the second you judge a new idea, you corrupt it, because judging is the rational mind's way of forcing one idea to agree with another. So as you can see, contemplation takes practice, and it takes humility.

Humility is the most important character trait you will develop. It begins with knowing that if a thing is real in the mind of God, it is a living entity with a life and mind of its own. Being humble means you have the ability to allow it to express itself. Only then can you truly know what it is and what it can become.

There is nothing new under the sun, but the possibilities are infinite. As we avail ourselves of that knowledge through the practice of meditation, we are changed, transformed from the inside out. And as we contemplate our inner experiences, we integrate them into our everyday lives. Thus we rise to ever higher states of being, knowing at all times that the engine of our progress is God, and God alone. We show up, but it is God who raises us up.

AN EXERCISE

Sit quietly in meditation and know that your mind is an extension of God's mind, and that it has direct access to that mind. Know that *that* mind is within you, not in some distant location, and know that you are within it. This is not difficult. The air you breathe is both outside of you and inside of you. And I don't mean just in your lungs. The air you breathe is literally in your cells, in the tiniest parts of you. The air you breathe becomes the tissues of your body. Think about the mind of God in this pervasive way.

Breathe slowly, deeply, and rhythmically. Let your thoughts coast gently to a stop. Orient your attention as though you were listening for a faint sound in the distance, only the "distance" is an inner space, the kind you might experience in a dream.

Be attentive to what you experience there, what you see, what you hear. Later, you will write these down in your journal. The language of the subconscious mind is symbols, and after you have finished with your meditation, you will want to examine them consciously and with respect.

Now, as though you were offering a gift to God on the altar, mentally elevate the pure concept of humility. I say "pure" as a way of saying that the concept of humility already exists in the mind of God, and that this is what you are asking, not what you already "know" about it. Forget what you've heard or read, even what you have read in this chapter. Let God show you what humility is.

What did you get?

Don't be concerned if nothing seems to happen. If your intention is intact, and you truly desire to receive, the knowledge will come through. It *has* to. God is incapable of holding back from a true request. You might not be conscious of the answer, but what does that matter? The effects of what you receive will emerge, sooner or later. To the degree that you *trust* that this will happen, it will happen. "Be it done unto you according to your [*trust*]."

When you are finished with your meditation, and after you have written down any pertinent thoughts, get up and do something else, something that will occupy your mind entirely, so that you forget about what you have just experienced. This is very important. As long as you are engaged with the process, it cannot begin its work inside you. You have to let it go, the same way you have to let go of a seed so that it can germinate. Let the experience fall into the fertile soil of your deep, inner consciousness. Do not try to dig it up later just to see if it's working. That would only interrupt the process.

How to Practice Humility

Humility is more than just a word. Humility is a state of being. Understanding what the word means helps us attain to that state of being, but we have to slip over from the concept to the reality.

The transition from concept to state of being is a process with many parts—components that exist in a dynamic relationship with each other. To attain to the humility state of being, we first examine its many parts individually, which unfortunately separates them from the whole.

We want our perception of God to be one of aliveness and the joyous interaction of life with life. So, remember this conceptual dissection for what it is, and try not to mistake the component parts for the dynamic whole.

The first component in the process of attaining to the humility state of being is practice. And there are several ways you can practice being humble. The first and easiest way is to approach other people as though they have something to teach you. No matter how smart you are or how spiritual you may feel, every person you meet will have a quality that is unique to them. No one else possesses their unique quality in the same way. Your job in this first step of the process of attaining humility is to identify that quality and to let it occupy a space in your awareness.

You have heard the saying that we are each created in the image and likeness of God. This image is alive and exists in a state of interaction with other created beings. Think about this. Every descriptor we have for God, in whose image we are created (e.g., love, life, light), implies interaction. Even the Holy Trinity divides God up into interactive, component parts, each of which is necessary to complete the whole.

So, when we look at others with an eye to their unique spiritual quality, we are looking at them as though they were God, as though they were plucked off of this planet and given a planet of their own, and we get to observe the nature and quality of their godhood. What unique personality would they bring to their planet? What would the people of that planet look like if the evolutionary goal they were striving toward had this same unique spiritual quality? How would the nature of life feel on their planet?

This is not as far-fetched as it might seem. For if we are in fact created in God's own image, then in an individualized sense we *are* gods. Our fundamental spiritual function is identical with that of this Great Being in which we live, move, and have our being. God's image and likeness is not anthropomorphic. It is spiritual. Our physical body is merely a vehicle that enables us to experience the physical world. The other dimensions of our being (e.g., mind, soul, and spirit) are the "source data" for all of its functions. God's image and likeness includes the entire spectrum of our existence, not just our flesh.

Exercising your awareness in this way will allow you to examine something in the other person that is very large, spiritually speaking. It is so large that you will find it worthy of your reverence. And in that moment you will be in the state of being called humility—you will be humble. And if you persist in this, you might get a glimpse of yourself and your own unique spiritual quality, which can be extraordinarily interesting and can lead to all kinds of spiritual awakenings.

But be careful not to use this as a way to categorize other people, or to manipulate them in any way. That would only degrade your ability to see the divinity in yourself, which would be tragic and very costly for you in your journey toward God-realization. Be aware also that seeing the deeper spiritual aspect of another person can potentialize your connection with them, and they will feel it. Do it too much and they might begin to mistrust you or misinterpret your feelings in other ways. Keep your observations brief, and ask God to bless each person you look upon in this way.

HUMILITY AND FORGIVNESS

The second component of humility is forgiveness. Forgiveness seems difficult because often it is confused with condoning the action that has harmed us. Or, we think that we are obliged to love the perpetrator as though "love" meant affectionate regard. These misunderstandings make forgiveness nearly impossible, if not downright repugnant. To forgive in these contexts would open us to charges of weakness and moral cowardice. So to appear strong, we cultivate hatred and thus lose our humanity.

The problem with condoning a harmful action or feeling affection for the perpetrator is that both of these postures are emotionally reactive. Siding with the wrongdoer is borne of fear—if I act like I'm one of them, maybe they will leave me alone. Or, if I pretend to like them, maybe they will like me back and stop hurting me. Both of these strategies give power away to the aggressor and can only perpetuate the problem. Therefore, they have nothing whatsoever to do with forgiveness.

The concept of forgiveness can also be misconstrued to mean excusing the malicious acts of another person, to simply overlook them as though they did not matter—to "rise above" them. But just as anger cannot be ignored or suppressed, neither can the negative traits of another be swept aside as though they did not exist.

Instead, they can be allowed to be what they are.

Instead of resisting what you do not like in the other person, give it space—allow it to be what it is. Give, as in *give way.* Do not resist—do not try to superimpose your sense of right and wrong onto the other person. If you do, you will always be disappointed, and eventually your disappointment will turn into indignation.

Indignation blinds us to what is and makes us ineffective. In the movie The Godfather, Michael Corleone says, "Never hate your enemy—it affects your judgment." We are offended by those things that reveal our own weaknesses. Real strength is never—*can never be*—offended. So look for the lesson. Let your adversary be your teacher.

This is the opposite of pressurizing or trying to contain what other people are putting out. Pressurizing them is the same as judging them; judgment is trying to force other people to be as you would have them be. No one responds well to that. Do you?

Forgiveness acknowledges that there is more to the other person than you are seeing and is therefore an aspect of humility. Carelessness, malice, greed, ignorance—these are all symptoms of deeper problems. We cannot ignore them, but we can look past them to see what is really there. The ego is always in competition with other egos. When we look for the divinity in the other person, we are bypassing his or her ego, and our indignation begins to fall away.

What can you accurately say about a violent person? What is the "what is" of him? Violence is the outgrowth of anger. Anger is the outgrowth of the sense of having been wronged. The sense of having been wronged is the outgrowth of the violation of a preconceived idea of how things should be. You might call this the *wounded wounder*—the human tendency to act out the abuses suffered earlier in life. This doesn't excuse bad behavior, but it does give us a way to understand it, and by understanding it we can deal with it more effectively.

By understanding bad behavior, we demon-
strate humility by putting our energy into effective action rather than letting it inflame our
already indignant ego.

Here is another way to understand a violent
person. Take, for example, the pathological killer.
When people are split within themselves, they
tend to see their separated part as the enemy. But
in their insanity, they are unable to understand
that their tormentor is a part of themselves, so
they project it outward onto other people. By
killing the other, they mistakenly believe that
they are killing the part of themselves that is
causing them pain. This is obviously insane, but
such is the belief of a fragmented personality.

This is why in hostage situations, hostages are
encouraged to talk to their abductors, to try to
get them to see that they are real people rather
than faceless, nameless "things" to be abused.
The more real the other person becomes in the
mind of the perpetrator, the harder it is to project
his inner demons upon them.

Again, this is not an excuse for deranged
behavior, but rather a way to understand and
thereby be more effective in one's response to a

dangerous situation. Sometimes that response is lethal force. When the perpetrator is so blinded by rage or so hardened in his heart that no amount of reasoning or caring can talk him down, he must be stopped by any means necessary, lest he cause more damage. But extreme situations are never isolated incidents. Rather they are the culmination of a long string of events, the fatal outcome of many mistakes made by everyone—you, me, the perpetrator, and society at large.

Until our collective consciousness expands to include an awareness of the seeds of problems, and our hearts develop to the point where we actually care about everyone and not just ourselves, we will continue to create an environment where human tragedy can flourish. No one is exempt from the chain of cause and effect. Action or inaction, knowledge or ignorance, zeal or apathy—the choice is always ours. Everything we do or not do, say or don't say, accept or reject shapes the world in which we live, and our wrongful choices will inevitably, as night follows day, come back to bite us.

Jesus said not to fear those who can kill your body but to be [damned afraid] of those who can cast your soul into hell. No one can cast our soul into hell, but they can induce us to do that to ourselves. And that is the danger Jesus warns us about. When we regard an insane person as an "evil" person, we start to hate him. Hatred is the "fires of hell." Hatred corrupts the hater, making him identical, spiritually speaking, to the object of his hatred. Science fiction author Frank Herbert once said, "We tend to become like the worst in those we oppose."

Mastering forgiveness does not mean there won't be a fight—it only enables you to keep a clear head. Never go into a fight blindfolded. The violent person believes that there is something wrong with the world and is attempting to fix it. If you know that, you are in a much better position to deal with him effectively.

According to George Lamsa, expert in Aramaic and Middle Eastern idioms, the saying, "Turn the other cheek," means "do not start a fight"—do not react. Reaction is powerless, because you are letting the other person state the terms of engagement. It is better to walk away and wait for the opportunity to begin a new round, one that will allow you to take the high ground.

Historically, the fiercest warriors have been the Samurai—the armies of the warlords of feudal Japan. The mythologist Joseph Campbell tells the story of one Samurai sent to avenge the murderer of his master. He takes the warlord by surprise, and just as he is about to cut off his head, the desperate warlord spits in his face. The Samurai warrior immediately sheaths his sword and walks away, leaving the warlord unharmed. Why? Because it is against the Samurai code of honor to kill in anger.

Forgiveness abates anger. And while anger can induce us to act, to pry us out of a rut, it must be quickly sublimated into willpower, or it will work against us and lead us into bigger problems.

Action is powerful when it operates at the level of cause. But re-action only gives power away. Reaction makes us want to hurt the other person back, instead of focusing our attention on taking an appropriate response. Turning the other cheek does not mean letting the other person continue to hurt you. What would be the purpose of that? Turning the other cheek simply means don't start a fight. It does not mean, however, that you can't *finish* one. Lashing back at our aggressor in the heat of the moment rarely if ever serves us well. A great example of this is in the movie *To Kill a Mockingbird,* when Atticus refrains from striking the man who spits in his face. Hitting him would not have served any purpose but to assuage his ego. Later, he wins the courtroom battle—he finishes the fight.

3

HUMILITY AND DIVINE GUIDANCE

The third component of the aspect of humility is divine guidance, the act of seeking direction in your life by asking God to reveal it to you.

But...a boat set adrift needs no guidance. It is not going anywhere in particular, so any direction will do. In life, it is better to pick a direction, any direction, engage your willpower, and then go for it. If it turns out to be the wrong direction, inner guidance will kick in and by degrees set you on a better course. But drifting will get you nowhere except by accident, and that's no way to live your life.

God is less spiritual than people make Him out to be. He's much more interested in sinners than He is in saints—not because He likes sin, but because He likes those who push against the boundaries and take risks. He likes people who are in action in their lives, because it is those people who *know what they want* . It is easier to help people get somewhere if they know where they want to go. Those who don't have a vision are usually sitting on their heart's desire, afraid to let it out, lest it disrupt their normal lives. There is no virtue in that. None at all.

So, if you want God's help, position yourself in such a way that you need it, need it like your body needs air. God can't help but join you in your endeavors, but you have to know what you want and be willing to stick your neck out to get it.

"Until one is committed, there is hesitancy, the chance to draw back, always ineffectiveness. Whatever you can do or dream you can, begin it. Boldness has genius, power, and magic in it."

DIVINE GUIDANCE AND DESIRE

The fourth component in the aspect of humility is desire. The very act of asking for divine guidance implies that we want something. So, desire is built into the system. It's what makes having goals possible. Desire is essential to the process of being guided. Desire is the motive force that propels us towards our goal, the very thing that causes us to ask for guidance in the first place.

But, you cannot want something for which you have no concept. Someone once said, "The eyes are the scouts of the heart." First the mind decides what it will value, then it uses the reports of the eyes to determine what it will go after. "Where your treasure is, there will your heart be also." You cannot want a thing unless you have the *idea* that it is valuable.

Why is this important? Unless you want something, you cannot receive guidance on how to get it. It's like the woman who was taken into an alien spaceship. She asked where its occupants had come from. She was shown a map of the galaxy and asked to point to the earth, which she could not do. The space beings replied, "If you don't know where you are, what does it matter where we are from?"

Usually, when we ask ourselves, "What do I want?" the question seems impossible to answer. So much rides on getting it right. And perhaps there is a bit of reluctance to ask for something for ourselves, which can feel a little selfish. So, there is a technique, a way to circumvent the anxiety and the guilt. Instead of asking "What do I want?" ask, "What do I *love*?" Guilt and anxiety cannot compete with your heart's desire.

What do you love? What, when you think about it, causes you to light up? What would you do if time and money were no object? Whatever that is, it's really non-negotiable. It is what you *have* to do. Of all the magnets you carry around with you in your heart, this is the one that has the most pull. It will cause the rocks and stones themselves to yell out the guidance you need.

What do you love? Until you know this, guidance will be hard to come by. But when you are honest with yourself and true to your first love, the entire universe will be at your service.

WHAT SHOULD YOU DESIRE?

No one can tell you what you should or should not want. It is simply none of their business. In fact, you cannot pick and choose your own desires, either. What you want lies deeper than your intellect. And it will not be denied.

Usually, we are afraid of our desires, because there are prohibitions against those urges we carry around within us—the urges of sex and pleasure, of wanting to stay home and watch television, to raid the refrigerator, to talk trash about the boss—anything and everything that goes against the hallowed Protestant work ethic stamped on our foreheads at birth. To give in to these is to shirk our responsibilities, to slide into a dissolute life, to waste the opportunity that life is.

But here is what we don't understand: the soul is deeper than the body, and all of the body's likes and dislikes mean nothing whatsoever to the soul. The soul craves for none of the things the body strains itself to get. But when we ignore the soul's desires, they come out twisted. The desire for love turns into uncontrollable lust; the desire for harmony turns into the need to control others; the desire to rise above the constraints of the world and soar in the realms of Spirit gets turned into fear of the unknown and the reluctance to engage with life. The body merely acts out the thwarted desires of the soul in the only way it knows how. Its ways are dictated by the need to survive, the need to take what it needs from its immediate environment, and the absolute necessity to dominate those with whom it must compete.

The soul cares nothing about these things.

The soul wants to give. It wants to connect with God and with other souls. If we stifle the soul's desires, if we ignore them and fall into the trap of believing that the earthly experience is the only reality and play only by *its* rules and not listen to the higher calling of our soul, then we enter into a death spiral that grows tighter and tighter until we can no longer breathe, and the fondest hopes of our heart begin to languish and slip into a dreamless sleep, waiting for another life where it might try again.

The answer is not to starve the body by forcing it to give up the things it wants. This has never been a workable strategy. As the French advertising guru Clotaire Rapaille once put it, "The spinal cord always wins." No, the body must be turned by degree, won over by love and consistent training, the same as you would train a horse. Try to coerce a horse to behave, and you will either cause it to rebel or you will break its spirit. Either way, it will be of no use to you and will only cause you trouble.

A horse is most valuable when it is allowed to *be* a horse. Horses love to run. Make it pull a plow all day or endlessly plod in front of a carriage, and you will blow out the fire in its heart. Your body is the same. If all you do is work, if all you do is think mundane thoughts, if all you do is relentlessly try to force the world to conform to your ideas of right and wrong, then you will extinguish the fires of the Spirit in your soul.

Where is the joy in your life? What is your life's upward trajectory? For what would you be willing to die, and to do so gladly? If you direct your attention to these inward qualities that make up the character of your soul, they will stream downward into your body and by degrees refine its senses and sensibilities. The body will become the vehicle it was meant to be and will cease being the unruly, rebellious child you have made of it.

Far from being the straight-jacket that most people believe vows to be, they are windows newly installed in the roof of our mind, windows that let the sunlight and fresh air into our daily experience. The vows are not there to make us feel bad when we do something wrong, but to continually pour in what is beautiful and right. They are the openings through which the contents of our higher mind can flow. How? By mirroring those divine thoughts and putting them into human terms.

To be humble is not to grovel but to make possible the experience of awe. It is *that* that is our soul's desire—to perceive the face of God.

A NOTE ABOUT DIVINE GUIDANCE

We want divine guidance, but we don't want to open up to just anyone. Just because we are able to get into a transcendent state of mind doesn't necessarily mean that we are communing with God. There are many levels of consciousness in the universal mind, and not all of them are reliable sources of truth. Some are misleading, some are irrelevant to our earthly life, and some are parasitic and should be avoided.

How are we to know the difference? How can we be sure that we are connecting with God and not some out-of-body, earthbound spirit? How can we be sure that the still, small voice we hear in meditation isn't our own mind spewing out unresolved, subconscious wishes or opinions?

These are important questions.

Instinctively, we know there are real risks involved in opening ourselves up to "higher guidance." It makes us cautious, and rightfully so. We have all seen people who, after flinging open the gates of their subconscious, are now wearing white jackets, the sleeves of which are tied behind their backs.

This is why devotion is an important part of our spiritual training and development. The heart must be oriented toward God, and the will must be conditioned to help us seek nothing less than the highest truth we are capable of conceiving.

When presented with an energy or spirit of unknown origin, always tell it to stand in the light of Christ. Be firm. Refuse to listen until you are sure it passes this test. Don't worry, it won't disappear if it's legitimate. In fact, you will get a lot more of it if you can prove that you won't fall for just anything. And if you're not sure what the light of Christ is, or you can't tell if it comes when you call upon it, get down on your knees and call it down on yourself. You'll know when it happens, because you will *feel* it. You will feel the Christ force clear the field around you and surround you with peace.

HUMILITY AND HONESTY

Another requisite component of the aspect of humility is honesty. And the person with whom we must be most honest is ourselves.

Our lives are plagued by mistakes. We make them all the time. We want God to tell us what to do. After all, God is all-knowing and all-wise, right? If we knew what God knows, we would never again make a mistake.

Why then is it so hard to get guidance from God? Why do some people get answers while others wander in the dark? What do they know that makes it so easy? If only we could tap into that! Perhaps the problem is in the way we approach God. In mock humility, we pretend that we don't want anything, as though we want God to tell us what to want. The truth is that we already know what we want, but we are afraid to admit it, even to ourselves. And when we do finally admit it, we turn it into shame. This is like trying to drive with the brakes on—lots of heat and no progress.

You cannot be a phony with God. You cannot pretend that you don't want something when you do. If you do pretend, you are only suppressing your desire, and nothing gets resolved.

And yet, this is exactly what Jesus promises us in the Bible. He said to ask for whatever we want and that God will give it to us, no questions asked. *Ask and it will be given to you; seek and you will find; knock and it will be opened to you.* No mixed messages here. And he didn't say that you had to be good enough, that you had to deserve God's help. He said nothing about that *at all.* God is not someone with whom you have to plead or bargain. God gives to whoever asks. *Whoever.* So, why is it so hard?

One way to understand how God works is to understand how you work. If you want to know why God answers the prayers of some people and not others, observe what you yourself do when people ask you for things. What makes you want to give to one person and not to another?

The main reason, I think you will find, is how clearly the person knows what he or she wants.

The second reason is how directly they ask. The man or woman standing on the street corner with a cardboard sign is far more likely to get a handout if they look you in the eye and ask for *your* help. There has to be a connection in order to motivate you to give. And while we do not want to approach God like a beggar, we can learn a lot about how asking works, why some requests get a response and others do not.

HUMILITY AND THE WILL OF GOD

According to conventional wisdom, humility is putting God's will ahead of our own. *This is a profound misunderstanding,* because there is no such thing as two separate wills. There is only one will. When we believe in two separate wills—ours and God's—it is only then that an opposition between them is possible. The reason we believe in two separate wills is that we allow our sense of self to compete with what needs to be done. We allow our considerations to get in the way, such as how we will look, what others will think of us, or whether there will be risks to our well being.

We exist in a living system wherein everything is connected in a constantly changing relationship with everything else. In the midst of constant change, the system tries to right itself moment by moment. And while the system is spiritually conscious and alive, it maintains its equilibrium automatically, just like the human body, and it does so without considerations.

Therein lies the difference between it and us— we are always taking into consideration how the change is going to affect our sense of self, whether it will reinforce it or undermine its current status.

Our sense of self is based upon the belief that we are a separate entity within the system, as though we were independent from the dynamic interplay of balance and change. Since we are biased toward the preservation of our sense of self, change appears as a threat, so we tend to resist it, opting instead for the safety of what is already known. As a coping mechanism, resisting change while living in a constantly changing system is unsustainable. But if we are stubborn enough, we can hold out for quite a long time, until the imbalance becomes so great that coming back into balance can bring with it a certain amount of violence.

Animals generally have no problem in adapting to changes in the system, because they do not have a sense of self that separates them from the whole. Even if the changes bring about their demise, there is no problem, because they do not see themselves as living outside of the system. The system is their home. We, on the other hand, do not feel that we belong here. The center of our lives is the mind, and that enables us to not only manipulate the system but to do so in ways that allow us to perpetuate our sense of self. We have the capability to establish ourselves as an independent agency within a system that cannot conceive of independence. This is an extremely dangerous situation, but at the same time, it is an extraordinary opportunity for self-discovery and exploration.

The danger is not only that we can disrupt the system, making it inhospitable to our very existence, but that it can lead us to imagine that we are immune to the consequences of our choices.

This is by far the greater danger. It leads to the philosophy that if something can be done, it *should* be done. It divorces knowledge from wisdom, leading to most of the problems we face today. The word for this dangerous mindset is "hubris"—excessive pride, or arrogance—the very opposite of humility.

However, if we had *no* pride, if we had no sense of self that enabled us to see ourselves as "not of this world," we would be the same as the animals—just another species of nature. We would have no ability to see the system objectively or manipulate it to our advantage. It's not that our choices would be limited, it's that we would have no choice whatsoever. We would only be able to do what the system allows us to do within the parameters of its own rules. There would be no creativity, no imagination, and no adaptability, except for a simple response to changes in the environment. We would have no ability to transcend our environment or to rise above that which nature has determined for us to be—simply a part of itself in its *un*-selfconscious automatism.

Clearly, surrendering to nature brings with it a profound sense of peace and contentment. Animals are entirely unconflicted about their place in the system. We, on the other hand, are deeply conflicted about our role here. We vacillate between wanting to go back to nature and boldly going where no one has gone before. We are cursed with the need to explore, the need to invent, the need to create. We are fascinated by the *new*, the different, the strange. We want to test ourselves, to explore our capabilities, to grow beyond our place in the system. We see the world as though it were a tomb from which we must resurrect.

We can no more ignore this about ourselves than we can ignore the basic needs of our animal nature. In fact, we are often torn between these two sets of needs, which are irrefutably at odds with each other. The one set is based entirely on survival, the other on the need to transcend. The one seeks the comfort and security of the known world, the other the forbidden territory of the mythological "north." The one seeks its identity in the group, the other in an unnamed calling that is deeply individual. Denying this second set of needs is tantamount to spiritual death. It leads to neuroses and physical disease. Our lifespans are not so much increased by advances in medicine as they are by expanding our horizons. The more we can envision the possible, the more fervently we want to live.

If we believe that our personal will is fundamentally different from God's will, we will always be trying to either fix it or to do away with it altogether. We would believe that there is nothing divine in us at all, that we were never created in God's image, that we are not a creator, and that we have no say about what happens in our lives. We would be like the animals, natural but unable to transcend nature.

When we read in Genesis that God gave man dominion over the earth and all its creatures, it means that the element of mind sets human beings apart from nature, freeing us from the blind machinations of the law of cause and effect. Through mind, we can initiate new causes and thereby chart our own course in our evolutionary path, albeit within the parameters of what we are able to conceive. This path, as mentioned before, is both extremely dangerous and an extra-

ordinary opportunity. It is dangerous because of
hubris—our unwillingness to listen to the voice
of wisdom, following instead the imaginings
of our ambitious sense of self. It is an opportunity
because we get to exercise our God-given creativity in ways we can't even envision. The possibilities for expression and self-knowing are
without limit.

Here we have to come to grips with our fali-
bility—our tendency to make mistakes. We have
to be able to be at peace with this if we are to progress further in our search for truth. Let us
imagine that eating the fruit of the Tree of the
Knowledge of Good and Evil was actually part of
the overall plan for the Human Project and that
having to find our own way in the world was an
integral part of our evolution. No mistake, no
original sin. After all, if God created us as free
agents, disobedience would be part of the program—an absolutely *necessary* part of the program, since unpredictabllility is an essential ingre-
dient of creativity. Why else would God have created humanity if not to explore the full range of
creativity inherent in the Creation? We are God's
creative agents in the world.

The tools God gave us with which to create are the Word of Power and the Law. The Word of Power is what makes it possible for us to *speak* the creation into being. And while our actual vocalisations have a certain amount of creative power, it is the roots of speech, namely *thought*, that has the real power to shape our experience in the world. It is our ability to think that has produced all that makes us uniquely human, for good or ill. And again, without the possibility for error, there can be no creativity. Risk, or *daring* , is a fundamental part of the creative process. "To will, to dare, to do, to be silent."

The Law is just another name for prayer. Not the *God, please give me* kind of prayer, but the *God, I ACCEPT this* kind . This is the kind of prayer that Jesus taught when he said, "Whatsoever you ask in prayer, believing, will be granted to you." If we really believe this, our knowing is complete. We have perfect confidence in our ability to call into manifestation whatever we want. The fact that we can also create problems for ourselves simply reiterates the fundamental role of the possibility for error in the creative process.

So, entertaining this idea that God created us specifically to leave Paradise and explore the creative potentials of this world, giving us the tools of creation that we would need in order to function as God functions, then the will of God could only be one thing—that we be creative, that we grow and develop the seeds of possibility hardwired into us from the beginning.

To think that God wants to direct our every move is the height of egotism. It is also a denial of our own God-given divinity, which more than anything else is what makes us human. Believing that God wants to manipulate us the way a puppeteer pulls the strings of a marionette is to deny the very purpose of our existence, namely to learn and to evolve—to reveal the nascent God within us, to become Sons and Daughters of the Most High.

It is a crushing blow to the ego to realize that God does not particularly care what we do with our lives—what job we have, what country we live in, what religion we belong to. God does not care about these things. God only cares that we use the tools that we were given, and that we use them *creatively*. This means that we are to explore and develop the inherent potential of all things, especially ourselves. And we are to do this in such a way that does not disrupt the systems of the world. To do so would be to defeat the purpose of the entire project—to raise the earth (and ourselves) to its highest level of expression. "Dominion over the earth" does not give us the right to kill it.

The only definitive thing we can say about God's will is that God wants us to use the tools we've been given to create the world we want to live in. That's all. There is no divine plan that specifies what the world should look like, what kind of governments we should have, what kind of religion everyone should follow. None of that. The only requirement is that we leave the place in better shape than we found it.

And here's the real kicker—*God does not know what the final product will be!* If God had known what the creative potential in human beings was going to deliver, there would have been no reason to create us. Unpredictability is the cornerstone of the creative act. It is, one might say, the whole point. Evidently, God likes a surprise as much as anyone.

If you can set aside what you already know about humility and look at it from this angle, you will see the enormous opportunity that God has made available to us for growth and spiritual development. There is nothing else like it. It is awe-inspiring. It takes real humility to take up the challenge God has given us—to accept our innate divinity and to use it to explore and develop the potential greatness of this world.

4

THE VOW OF POVERTY AND THE PRINCIPLE OF NON-ATTACHMENT

When thinking of the vow of poverty, an image leaps to mind, and it is an image that you will find highly improbable if not downright ridiculous. The image is from a scene in the sci-fi movie *Terminator 2: Judgement Day*. (See, I told you!)

Here's the story: Sarah Connor is on a mission to assassinate the scientist who will eventually create the artificial intelligence that in the future will seek to eradicate humanity. She knows this because others have travelled back in time to tell her how it will all play out. They come to her because she is the mother of John Connor, the future leader of the resistance against the machines. So, in her role as the mother of the messiah, she spends the years leading up to Armageddon in combat training. (I'm telling you this just in case you are one of the three people alive today who are unfamiliar with the story.)

So, this is the scene: It is nighttime. Sarah Connor is in camouflage and armed with an assault rifle with a night-vision, laser-guided scope, and a sidearm. Her target is seated at his computer unwittingly engineering the destruction of the human race. She is positioning the little red dot on the back of his head from her vantage point outside, and just as she is about to pull the trigger and save the world, the scientist bends down to reach for something. Her sniper round clinks through the window glass and shatters his computer monitor. He is immediately alerted to the imminent danger and heads for shelter away from the windows and into the interior of the house.

Sarah, as I'm sure *you* would, realizes that her assault rifle will be cumbersome in close-quarters. So, without hesitation she throws it down on the ground and unholsters her automatic. She is intensely focused and disciplined in the pursuit of her target. Now this is the part that speaks volumes to me about the vow of poverty, specifically the part where she *throws her rifle down on the ground.* When I saw her do that, my first thought was, "O my god, that's got to be at least $3,000 worth of equipment she just dropped in the dirt! I mean, couldn't she have carefully set it down, on the grass maybe?" No. She discards it as if it were the one thing keeping her from her goal—a thing vile, to be despised, so worthless as to be hateful. She shed that gun as though it were a T-shirt stained with cranberry juice.

And there's this other thing, and I promise to get right back to Sarah, because I know you're dying to know what happens next, but this is also germane to the point I'm trying to make. It was in traffic school (yes, I went to traffic school). The instructor said that one of the main causes of traffic accidents is eating while driving—that when faced with the decision of either hanging onto your Big Mac or grabbing your steering wheel, you will hang onto your Big Mac. I thought that was absurd, but it turns out to be true. It's kinda like the monkey that won't let go of the morsel inside the coconut shell, but because his hand will fit through the hole but his clenched fist won't, he's trapped and gets hauled off to the research lab.

Back to Sarah. When she realizes she's going to have to chase this guy through hallways and bedrooms, she flings her $3,000 rifle with nightvision, laser guided scope to the ground like it was *nothing* and leaves it forever. This was attributable, no doubt, to her rigorous combat training, which says that while your rifle is your best friend, it can quickly become your worst enemy, if trying to keep from getting a scratch on it causes you to hesitate at a critical moment.

Life is full of such choices. But the combat training we are interested in is the inner kind. What are we hanging onto that is getting in the way of the spiritual goals we have set for ourselves? Is it a house, a job, the opinions of others?

Some say that the vow of poverty is a way to facilitate communal living, as in a monastery. No one owns anything; all goods are shared amongst the community members as a way to foster harmony and cooperation. Others say that it is the Western equivalent of the Eastern principle of non-attachment, and while that is true, as an explanation it fails to provide us with a *purpose*. Why is non-attachment a good thing?

This is where Sarah has a lot to teach us. Her training has enabled her to be intensely focused. But is focus in and of itself the goal? Is non-attachment in and of itself spiritually viable? Non-attachment and the vow of poverty are tools, not goals. Once they achieve their purpose, they can be discarded, just as Sarah discarded her $3,000 rifle. Attachment is what the physical body is good at, and for its purposes that works well. But the spiritual path demands a certain mastery over the body, and *non*-attachment works well for that.

Too often the spiritual path gets turned into The Destination, a kind of religion in itself. This is a mistake. We need to stay two steps ahead of our religion at all times. As Jesus said, "The sabbath was made for man, not man for the sabbath." If you are stuck in the mindset that the spiritual path, however that might look for you, is

where you *have to be*, then when moments of lib-
eration lift you above the Earth, you will feel like
you are doing something wrong, that you are
being unfaithful. Don't spoil the moment. Let
tools be tools, and when they are no longer
needed, cast them aside. Do what Sarah did. This
is the heart of the vow of poverty.

NON-ATTACHMENT AS A STRATEGY FOR SUCCESS

House painters and furniture refinishers will
tell you that preparation is everything. Applying a
coat of paint or lacquer is easy. But the material
you lay down can only be as good as the surface
you lay it on. No amount of paint will adequately
cover a cracked and peeling surface.

The paint in this analogy is our efforts to make
ourselves look good. I'm not talking about taking
care of our appearance or keeping up the condition of our home, dressing our children properly,
etc. I have a friend who likes to say, "Look sharp,
feel sharp, *be* sharp." He always dresses well, his
home is clean and orderly, and his mind reflects
the care he puts into his surroundings. He does
this to be sharp, not to look good. He does it for
the effect it has on *him*, not the effect it has on
others. Keeping himself sharp is his preparation

for all of the other things in his life. Being sharp keeps him ready.

When we have a goal in life, we naturally want to reach it. False notions about the vow of poverty can hold us back unnecessarily. Having possessions, having lots of money, and having a lifestyle that some might call lavish do not of themselves negate the principle of non-attachment. Being non-attached simply means that we do not put things ahead of our goals. And we do not make the focus of our life the acquisition of things. Spirit is action. To lead a spiritual life, we must place activity at the center of our aspirations. Our purpose in life is to do and to be, not to have.

As a general rule, it is always better to only keep those things that are either useful and/or enjoyable. If you hang onto stuff from the past, it is quite likely that you are having trouble letting go. Failing to let go is one of the biggest stumbling blocks on the spiritual path. If you are hoarding stuff in case you might need it in the future, you are actively saying that you do not trust God to provide the things you need as you need them. Hoarding is anti-faith.

So, we don't need to live like monks in a monastery, possessing only a begging bowl and a loin-
cloth or a robe and set of rosary beads. Everyday
life demands that we engage with the world, and
that takes stuff. As long as our stuff doesn't prevent us from engaging with the world in a way
that helps us reach our spiritual goals, then it
doesn't matter what stuff we have. We are free to
choose the things in our lives.

From The Bhagavad Gita:

*One who shirks action does not attain freedom;
no one can gain perfection by abstaining from work.
Indeed, there is no one who rests for even an instant;
all creatures are driven to action by their own
nature.*

Remember, the Five Vows are empowering,
not restrictive. They make us more effective *in
the world*. What good is a spiritual life if it is not
expressed here and now? It is only by living the
truth that we are transformed. No one has ever
been transformed by a philosophy.

POVERTY AND THE ENGINES OF OUR LIFE

We now know that vows are more than a ritual,
more than a promise or declaration of intention.

We know that they are preexisting states of consciousness that we enter into. But if we say that poverty is an aspect of *God's* consciousness, we make God something external and different from ourselves. If we say that we *are* God, then the states of consciousness begin to feel like personal constructs—merely ideas having nothing to do with power, energy, and force. No cause, no effect—just bubbles in the bathtub of our mind.

But those of us who have lived with vows know that they are real, that they have real effects in our lives, that life would be different without them. This is why we study them, to try to understand what it is that we are experiencing. What is it about taking vows that puts our life on a different trajectory than if we had not taken them?

Mark Twain said, "Money isn't everything, as long as you have enough of it." No one is more obsessed with money than a person who has too little. But, as with all the vows, the vow of poverty is about something deeper, something universal. It's not about money. As we saw with Sarah Connor, it is a state of mind, a level of training, an unwillingness to let any *thing* get in the way of our connection with God.

Let's look at one more aspect of this:

Non-attachment is a tricky concept. Wrongly understood, it can lead a spiritual seeker to drift untethered across the vast open spaces of the mind. The subtle distinction is this: Because it is human nature to prefer to set our own course, we have a reluctance to be led. We might say that we want to surrender to God's will, but when it comes to actually doing it, well, that's another story. We always want to have the last word, to engineer our own destiny. This is why we are so obsessed with money, because money is power, and power is freedom.

The idea of being led is carefully woven into the words we use for spirituality. The word *yoga* comes from the Sanskrit word *yug*, meaning "yoke." The image is of two oxen yoked together, suggesting the union of opposites, but this is a misreading of the idea. The ox is a symbol of power—divine power—stemming from the Age of Taurus when this symbol was first used. The idea is to tether yourself to the oxen, to the divine power, and let it pull you along. Metaphorically speaking, most of us get through life by pushing our carts from behind, trying to do it all ourselves, as though personal effort were the highest virtue. But on the spiritual path, the only effort required is the willingness to let go and let God.

Here's one way you can get what it means to let go and let God. Most people tense up when driving up a steep hill, as though they have to help the car by gripping the steering wheel harder and by squeezing their stomach muscles, right? These contortions have absolutely no effect on whether the car will reach the top of the hill. The only effort we have to exert is the tiny bit of pressure required to depress the accelerator pedal and a gentle grip on the steering wheel. That's all. The car is doing the work, not you.

In order for a car to be reliable, we have to keep it in good condition. In everyday life, there are many kinds of *engines* we use to reach our goals, engines that require little more from us than a little confident steering and some watchful maintenance. One such engine is communication. Many of life's problems can be traced back to a lack of it. Staying in touch, checking in, asking questions, and answering them keeps the power flowing in our relationships.

Another engine is our investments. No amount of worry will cause a portfolio to increase in value. Most successful investors tell us to make a plan and stick to it. If we don't stick to our plan, we wind up chasing the market, trying to anticipate its short-term moves, and we start to lose money. Instead of letting the money work for us, we try to push the car up the hill.

I use these examples to show that the spiritual principle of non-attachment does not mean *non-engagement* with life. It does not mean that you cannot own anything or have lots of useful possessions.   Poverty—non-attachment—means that once you have set the engines in your life in motion and they are doing the work you intend for them to do, keep your hands off! Don't, as they say, "push the river." People who have mastered this seem to live their life with a graceful ease. They always have what they need, and the people and projects in their life *thrive.*

A light hand

As a spiritual principle, poverty is an attitude, not an inventory list. It is a style of living, an understanding that you have to let the constructive forces in your life work for you without your interference. Non-attachment is a light hand, an easy touch, not a death grip. When we get good at non-attachment, when we develop it as we would any other skill, we can better evaluate the viability of our projects, our entrepreneurial pursuits, our children, and every other living thing in our life. When something has a life of its own, even if we created it—*especially* if we created it— we have to let it find its own way. We can guide, we can steer, but we must not push. If we inject our own energies into a system, we can easily think that it has a pulse, when actually we are merely sensing our own heartbeat. The minute we try to let it stand on its own, it dies.

Non-attachment is essential in business and in life. You wind it up and you *let it go!* Hanging on and pushing every inch of the way only leads to disaster. It makes you tense and prone to making mistakes. It also blocks the valuable input of those around you. Let the energies in your life express themselves. After all, you put them there. Now let them work—*for you.*

Another word we use to describe spirituality is the word "religion." Like "yoga," it also refers to tethering. The Latin root of this word is *ligare*, which is the same root for the word "ligament." Ligaments connect bones to muscles, another form of motive power.

Tethering is different from binding. Binding feels like bondage, whereas tethering empowers. We tether a computer to a cell phone in order to go online without an Internet connection. We tether a dingy to a boat, or a horse to another horse. The purpose is to accomplish something, not to restrict—to perform an action, not to prevent an action.

Too often, vows are seen as binding restrictions and not as agents of empowerment, which is what they are. Jesus said, "Very truly I tell you, when you were younger you dressed yourself and went where you wanted; but when you are old you will stretch out your hands, and someone else will dress you and lead you where you do not want to go." Symbolically, the "young" person is he or she new to the path; the "old" person is one who is spiritually advanced and is able, even over the objections of his or her preferences, to be led by the Spirit. We follow our inner guidance, even when we don't feel like it. We say to God, "Take these hands and use them." This is the mark of spiritual maturity.

The best investments we can make are investments in ourselves. Rather than a boat in the driveway, we learn to play a musical instrument. Rather than more stuff, we hone our talents or develop new ones. This is true wealth, the kind we *can* take with us. Compassion, generosity, an affinity with God—these are possessions of the soul. No one can take these from us. But, the more encumbered we are by the things of this world, including ideas and opinions, sentiments and desires, the less able we are to be led by the Spirit. This is true impoverishment and the source of sorrow.

RUTHLESS POVERTY

Many motion pictures use myths as the basis of their story line, and *Terminator 2* is a good example. And since poverty is a spiritual principle, it's an easy bet that it will show up, as it does in this movie.

Since Sarah is The Mother, she represents the Divine Feminine—conserving, protecting, ruthless. Her level of horror at the impending nuclear holocaust personifies the raw survival instinct that will stop at nothing to preserve life. No *thing* gets in her way.

The Divine Feminine is the sharp end of the stick in the preservation of life department. She is red in tooth and claw—she will not hesitate to cull the herd if it means preserving the species.

The intellect of man is just the opposite: his rapacious need for more and more stuff willingly risks the entire ecosystem, destroying whole species, nearly on a daily basis. The mind of man *ignores* the heart of nature and is willing to die so that he might achieve the last thrust of his gluttony. With man, everything is external and temporary. Nature, however, takes a longer view.

Nature is less attached to form than she is to *systems*. Life is always changing its forms, always evolving, shedding its skin in order to adapt. Nature is relentless in her attachment to life, but she is the epitome of non-attachment when it comes to forms. Murdering an individual form is nothing compared with killing an entire system.

Poverty is stripped down; it is the consciousness of the essential. Poverty says, "Take everything you need, but no more." Nature's abundance is geared not only to the *what* but also to the *when*. A thing taken at the wrong time is taken not out of need but out of fear. And fear kills life—it shuts it down. Fear of lack stops the flow. One who has adapted to the consciousness of the essential never lacks for anything. Poverty leads to abundance. And it is the seed bed of generosity.

The vow of poverty leads one into the consciousness of the essential. A clear signal is a strong signal. Simplicity, clarity, focus—these are the footprints of poverty. When you find them, watch out! Because you're on the trail of a very powerful animal.

POVERTY AND GENEROSITY

The spiritual part of us thrives on giving. We have to give in order to live. The vow of poverty, when understood as non-attachment, frees us up to give generously of ourselves. When we are unconcerned with our self-image or how others see us, we can give more freely when giving is required. We can more easily say what needs to be said. We can risk looking foolish, because we are not attached to the opinions of others or some preconception of who we are supposed to be. A generous spirit is a powerful spirit, and when we are generous, we can be a force for good in the world.

When we understand that poverty as a spiritual principle is about non-attachment and not about wealth, we become better problem solvers. We are not as likely to try to fix people or situations by throwing money at them. Instead, we look for the roots of the problem, the underlying principle, the cause. Problems are almost never caused by a lack of stuff; the lack of stuff is the result, not the cause. We know that merely changing the effects will not have any lasting effect, if we do not find out what caused the problem in the first place.

If stuff were the solution to the problem, then we would have cause to worry, because stuff is finite. But when we realize that the cause is spiritual, there is hope, because Spirit is infinite— there is no limit to our ability to change our inner state. Our inner state is completely under our control, and it is our inner state that determines the conditions of our outer lives.

When we cannot be distracted by outer conditions, when we live in the state of consciousness that every *thing* is temporary, hanging onto stuff (our stuff, their stuff, the world's stuff) becomes impossible. And if we're not hanging onto it, we're not as inclined to hoard it or to think that we can solve problems by redistributing it. Too often, stuff is the primary goal in life, and *that's* the problem. When we let go of our attachment to stuff, we free up the Spirit so it can work in our life and the lives of others. Generosity becomes our default setting, and the stuff of the world naturally flows to where it's needed.

We're talking about a fundamental change in consciousness, one that the vow of poverty makes possible, or at least a lot easier to attain. It places being and activity at the center of our lives, not the acquisition of things and ideas. After all, what good is an idea if you can't use it?

Non-Attachment and Transformation

Non-attachment is about control. A woman mystic I know says, "We are either a yes or a no, and that's *all* we are."

By controlling our yeses and our nos, we steer our lives. We cannot override the accumulation of all that has gone before, except by the remedial action of reversing old choices with new ones. But it's the choices that are under our control, not the outer circumstances. We cannot change our world by rearranging its pieces, but we can facilitate its change by adding what's needed and eliminating what's not. But we cannot do this if we are attached to it all.

We are the center of our own solar system, the power source that keeps the swirl of our circumstances in orbit. We cannot effect changes in the swirl except by changing ourselves. We change our thoughts, our habits, our actions, and our character. To do this, we have to keep our attention on these inner aspects of ourselves, not the swirl. As *we* change, the swirl changes. It has to. But if the changes capture our attention and make us afraid of losing something, we will try to hold the swirl in place. This, as you might expect, will cause it to fly apart.

Taking the vow of poverty helps us to keep our focus on the inner aspects of our lives instead of always focusing on the things and circumstances that constantly surround us. This is what Jesus meant when he said to store up our treasures in heaven and not on Earth. He didn't mean that we had to deny ourselves earthly possessions or pleasures, as though doing that would store up cosmic credits that we could cash in after we die. That idea is nothing more than materialism dressed up for church. What he meant was that if we take care of our inner state, our outer state will take care of itself.

Of course, our inner state is what lives on after we die, and that is certainly important, but it doesn't mean we have to artificially suffer here in this world. Often, what leads us into negative situations is the cynicism that we adopt in our thinking, the cynicism that says there is no good in the world. We become resigned to the apparent evil until it becomes the very basis of our beliefs. Cynicism becomes the magnet that draws its characteristic experiences into our lives. "As a man thinketh in his heart, so is he." We can only see the world through our conceptual framework, and we can only grasp what we can see.

The vow of poverty empowers us in our living; it doesn't deprive us of the things we need in order to have a fulfilling life. It is a way of keeping our priorities straight, not a way of keeping our pockets empty.

5

THE VOW OF SERVICE— DELIBERATE LOVE

You may be noticing a pattern by now. Much of what we have said about the vow of poverty sounds a lot like the vow of humility. Letting go and letting God, the willingness to be led, recognizing that we don't own anything anyway—these are all aspects of humility. It's almost as though the five vows form a pyramid, with humility as its capstone.

In sacred symbology, five is the number of man and is represented by the five-pointed star. Humility is at the top, at the Crown Chakra, because to be humble is to be receptive. The left hand is the hand of receiving, and the right hand is the hand of giving. Hence we have, "Let not the right hand know what the left hand is doing"— don't give with an eye to what you might receive in return, but rather give without thought of repayment. This also relates to the vow of purity, but we will get to that later. For now, let's look at the right hand, the hand of giving: service.

The split between heart and brain is well known. And while we have the capacity to love, few of us can direct it. We can direct our attention, if we've developed the ability to concentrate, but we have a hard time summoning love when it is not already there. In other words, we find it difficult to love *deliberately*. This is at the heart of Jesus' words, "If you love those who love you, what reward will you get? Are not even the tax collectors doing that? And if you greet only your own people, what are you doing more than others? Do not even pagans do that? Be perfect, therefore, as your heavenly Father is perfect."

How many people in the world suffer from the condition known as failure to thrive? In a hospital study a few years back, it was discovered that touch—warm, affectionate human contact—was essential to premature babies in order for them to thrive. (See how long it takes for the mind to catch up to the heart?) Those who received it did well; those who didn't usually did not survive. Much of the trouble in the world can be directly traced to the lack of deliberate love. It is the one thing we all need—if not actual touch, then warm, affectionate regard. After all, we touch each other all the time with our minds.

At its core, service is about deliberate love. Moral conscience evolves from acting morally to thinking morally to *being* moral.

It takes courage to act morally, to do the right thing, to love deliberately. Why is it that some people can walk down the street through the most dangerous situations and not get accosted? It is because they do not judge those they see there. Judgement is the highest form of disservice there is, because it is an attempt to trap the other person in his error. Judgement says, "*You* are evil," when that person's soul knows that it is not. Don't be the person who tries to kill people's souls by condemning them to their error.

To serve is to exercise the heart. It is to love deliberately and then act accordingly. Deliberate love lacks sentimentality; it loves whether it feels like it or not. It loves not according to a set of standards but according to what the other person needs. We don't love only those who love us, those who are like us. We love anyone who needs love. And that includes everyone.

Nothing cleans the pipes of the heart like deliberate love, because deliberate love is powered by will. If we are always seeking to be loved by others, we will quickly lose the ability to discriminate between love and that which is not love. We will draw to ourselves all manner of "unclean spirits," as it says in the Bible. Desire is a vacuum, and there is no greater desire than the desire for love. Only by practicing love, by loving deliberately, can we remain clear about what love is and what it is not.

Giving love

The heart has been largely corrupted by selfishness and vanity. Living in a me-centered world can cause the ability to give love to atrophy. This is why charity work is so important to one's spiritual growth. Giving money to charities is not enough; you need to be personally involved. If you don't have time to spare, then you have to work charity into your every day living—into your job, your free time, your relationships. This is something we all need to do anyway, but the demands of daily life can be overwhelming, so we need to make the extra effort to make sure the giving aspect of our heart doesn't shut down.

This giving aspect is the difference between loving and wanting to be loved. Both are legitimate needs, but to be healthy, they must be kept in balance. They don't aways have to have an equal charge, but they need to stay within a dynamic range that allows for the full expression of both. Since the predominant mood of the world is fear, we can assume that our default setting is looking out for number one. We have to consciously override this innate tendency by planning and executing charitable acts, and we have to discipline ourselves to carry them out regardless of how we feel in the moment.

This is why there is such a lack of moral courage in the world. As a society, we seem to be losing the ability to know the difference between right and wrong. Looking out for number one has become the new moral standard. While not everyone subscribes to this belief, it is slowly working its way into the mainstream, if not by greed then by necessity. Those who have want more, and those who don't have will get what they need by any means necessary. This is spiritually dangerous, because it is an expression of fear, not love.

By recognizing that we have this tendency hardwired into us, we must be vigilant about how we interpret world events. If our perception of the world becomes more and more colored by what we interpret as rampant injustice, we will feel justified in taking back what was taken from us. If we see our employer as greedy and heartless, we are much more likely to take from him what we believe to be rightfully ours. This quickly puts us in the red, spiritually speaking. We become like the very thing we hate.

The only way to short-circuit this process is to give back more than we receive—"And whosoever shall compel thee to go a mile, go with him twain." Our willingness to give must always stay out ahead of our demands to be paid. Otherwise, we fall into the same trap that plagued Soviet society under the oppressive bureaucracy of the Communist Party. The Russian people would laugh and say, "They pretend to pay us, and we pretend to work." What good does it do to fight injustice if you wind up murdering your ability to give?

We must always work toward social and economic equality—equality under the law and equal access to the marketplace. This is our duty as conscious citizens, our service to the greater good. This is especially pertinent right now to the spiritual life, because the issue of global economic inequality is causing much unrest in the collective mind. Unless we find a way to engage with this problem in practical ways, the stress caused by doing nothing will eat us alive!

Whether we engage in political activism, or we simply vote with our pocketbook doesn't really matter, as long as we keep our thoughts and actions positive. How? By listening to the other side, by acknowledging that our adversary also has a point of view, which is as equally valid to him as ours is to us. If we fail to do this, we attempt to trap him in his error, a move that will make him want to fight us to the death. We must respect those with whom we disagree, even as we would have them respect us.

This is what it means to love our enemies. We love them by taking them seriously, not by demonizing them or discounting their concerns. We have to deliberately choose to respect the other side, knowing that respect means not scoffing at their beliefs. It's an act of will. It is deliberate. This is how we strengthen our heart and develop our moral courage. If the right hand is the hand of giving, then loving deliberately is "sitting at the right hand of God."

RIGHT ACTION AND ASKING

It's naive to think that service means doing whatever *we* think needs to be done. This has caused much of the suffering in the world throughout history. No one knows with certainty what needs doing. If we act according to *our* ideas of right and wrong, then our actions will likely be inappropriate. Even if we do know what another person needs, unless he needs it *now,* and unless he needs it *from us,* anything we attempt to give him will most likely cause him more harm than good. If we are to live up to our vow of service, we must learn to listen more to the Spirit and less to our own mind. Our mind might know the facts, but the Spirit within us is wise.

Action from wisdom is right action.

However, what may be right action in this moment may be disastrous in the next, because timing is everything. Knowing what to give is one thing; knowing *when* to give it is quite another. The perfect word spoken a moment too late can have the opposite effect of what we intended. But the right word spoken with perfect timing has the power to move mountains.

The intellect cannot know when a person is ready to hear what you have to say. The best that the mind can do is guess. It might know all the options, but it cannot tell which option is the right option at any given moment. Good timing does not come from the mind. It has to be felt. And by "feeling," I do not mean emotion. Emotions are phenomena of the physical world. They are instinctual. And unless you are an actor who has mastered the art of summoning emotions at will, they only come as responses to external circumstances, which is to say, they are reactive. The Spirit does not react, it *acts*.

Nor is the heart, strictly speaking, capable of executing right action, because withholding is not in its nature. Sometimes, right action requires *not* giving. The heart wants to give all the time, so it cannot be relied upon to make the right decisions when presented with a situation of need. Only the Spirit has perfect timing. Only the Spirit knows when and how much to give. The heart, like the mind, is a servant to the Spirit. It adds feeling and warmth. But only the Spirit can execute right action.

Like electricity, Spirit (the *power* of God) flows in the direction of need. But also like electricity, there has to be a difference in potential before a current will flow. The living symbol of this difference in potential is the act of kneeling in prayer. We assume a position of helplessness and surrender, putting ourselves in a lower position, symbolizing our inner state of submission to God's will. Symbolic action such as kneeling is powerful when performed consciously and with understanding. Kneeling is the physical expression of *asking*.

Often, in our desire to serve others, we attempt to impose our will where no request has been made. Thinking that we are wise in our dispassionate objectivity, we assume to know more about the power of God than God does. Trying to give when there has been no request has the effect of running an extension cord out of one wall socket into another. All you will get is a lot of sparks and possibly a fire. It is far better, when attempting to respond to a request, to *feel* the energy. Let it show you where it wants to go.

The best teachers teach by raising a question in the minds of their students. Unless and until there is a question, nothing is going to get in—the ego will simply not permit it. Similarly, unless people ask for your help, don't try to serve them. They will only find your attempts annoying. The highest form of service you can offer is to get in touch with the God of you—which is also the God of them—and present yourself as a conduit of grace. And if the person requests it, and if you are so inclined, you can lay your hands on him and give him a healing, thus giving the world of Spirit and the world of Matter a way to more intimately connect.

In order to have right action, a request must be made. You can only truly help people when they ask for it. But sometimes their request isn't obvious. Sometimes, it can be an unspoken request. This is why we must learn how to be in touch with the Spirit of God within us. We have to know what It knows. Only then can we be truly helpful. Only then can we truly serve. Stepping into the consciousness of service primes the pump for this kind of direct knowing. By taking the vow of service, we align ourselves with Spirit. Life is a force, and when we align ourselves with it, it will show us the direction in which *it* wants to move.

THE ART OF DOING NOTHING

We cannot truly be of service to another person until we master the art of doing nothing. It's easy to jump in and provide what we think is needed, but the world groans under the weight of such good intentions—people and institutions doing what's "best" for the poor unfortunates around them. More often than not, our good deeds miss the mark, and we wind up doing more harm than good. Our blunderings make us spiritually deaf and blind, and our failed attempts to fix the world can make us cynical. We become jaded and, eventually, we can grow to hate those who stubbornly refuse to accept our wisdom and benevolence.

Too often, we think we perceive a vacuum in other people, and we rush to fill it with what we think they need. This is the very opposite of being nurturing. The need is there, obviously, but if we assume we know what it is, we only set the stage for disaster. We only have to look at the many examples of missionary zeal throughout history to see the wreckage left in the wake of those who sought to save others.

The problem lies not in the other person but in ourselves. The vacuum is in *us*. Saint Francis said, "O Divine Master, grant that I may not so much seek…to be understood, as to understand." Nothing needs to be added, only revealed. In fact, until we know what is already there in people, it is impossible to give them what they need, because *we don't know what that is!*

Usually, the most helpful thing we can do for a person in trouble is to listen. The best service we can offer in a storm is a safe harbor.

The truest thing that can be said about human nature is that no one receives anything unless they ask for it. Why? Because unless they ask, they are not ready to accept. Unless there's a vacuum, nothing substantial can move in to fill it.

Surely, there are laws of physics at play here, but this is more easily understood through feeling than by thinking.

The key lies in knowing that everyone already knows what they need. The answers they seek are already there inside of them. What they need is our permission to let them out. By this, I mean that instead of trying to *give* them something, the best thing we can do is to back off—give them room to express the hidden thing. Depressurize them, so that what is scratching at the inside of the egg can break free. But backing off does not mean leaving—you have to *be there*. Be there and yet do nothing. This is why doing nothing is an art.

This is where the vow of service most closely mirrors the vow of humility. Again, all of the vows seem to be subsets of this one vow. The quality of humility is preeminent in all of the world's enduring faiths. The word "Muslim," for instance, means "one who submits." Mindfulness means to "just be with what is present." Namaste means "I salute the God within you." They all point to allowing people to be what they are. Once the energy starts moving in that direction

—from the center of their being outward—all of the imbalances can begin to heal. This happens from the inside out. Nothing we can add will be of any help.

PAYING ATTENTION

Spiritual truth is upside-down and backwards to what is true in the world. For instance, it's true that in order to live we must take our nourishment from the world. (Notice the word "take.") Every living thing eats, and eating is taking. That's how life survives in this world. But spiritually it is exactly the opposite. In order to thrive spiritually, we must *give*. Giving is essential for a healthy spiritual life.

Those who are in business for themselves know that in order for a company to survive, it must make a profit. No one stays in business for long if the money they take in only covers salaries and the bills. Conversely, in order to thrive spiritually, we must always give more than we receive. Giving more than we receive is spiritual profitability.

Giving is the life blood of a spiritual life. But it's how we give that's important, not so much what we give. Many people convince themselves that giving feels good and that this is the primary reason for doing it. But sometimes giving doesn't feel good; it just feels necessary. It may even hurt. So, it's important to remember that when we give, it's not for us—it's for the *other* person.

Sayings like "Give from the heart" and "The Lord loves a cheerful giver" do not explain how giving works. These sayings are little more than platitudes. To understand the underlying principle of giving, we have to look at it in terms of energy. And the primary form of energy that we have to work with is our attention. Our attention is either on the other person and what he or she needs, or it is on ourselves and what other people are thinking of us. In other words, we are either paying attention, or we are seeking it.

In terms of polarity, paying attention is positive, and seeking attention is negative. In paying attention, the energy is flowing outward, giving life to the world. In seeking attention, the energy is flowing inward, feeding our egos. Positive energy broadcasts—it radiates. Negative energy gathers—it takes for itself. To take an example from nature, solar energy is positive and gravity is negative. (The terms "positive" and "negative" in this context have nothing to do with good and bad.)

However, there are times when seeking energy, or even demanding it, is spiritually correct, especially if you need to lead others or organize a group project. But if we are honest with ourselves, we know that we are usually out of balance in this regard, constantly complaining about the conditions in our lives, who has treated us badly, and why we deserve much more than we are getting. So, to compensate for being out of balance, we need to forget about ourselves for awhile and give without regard for what we get in return. This is called *selfless service*, and it's the the key to spiritual growth.

In order to gain traction on the spiritual path, we must put into practice what we learn intellectually. Otherwise, it does us no good whatsoever. We would be better off studying how to succeed in the world, how to lose weight, or how to find the perfect partner. None of these things will help us grow spiritually, however, because the energy involved in these pursuits is negative—it's all for us. So, practice is anything we do that takes our attention off of ourselves and places it on other people and what *they* need. Sometimes, simply appreciating them for who they are can give them the space they need to express themselves positively or creatively. This can help them turn their energy around rather than spend all of their time trying to get something for themselves. But in order for this to work, we should avoid preaching to them. Preaching has the opposite effect, because when we're talking, we aren't listening. And listening is what paying attention is all about.

Caveat: Paying attention to other people is different than placing expectations on them. When we do that, our energy switches back to negative, because we are trying to get them to give us a certain kind of behavior. So, truly paying attention requires a non-judgmental frame of mind. We have to be willing to accept other people as they are, with a mind to what they might become, but without putting any stipulations on what that might be.

Attention is energy. Giving it gives energy to others. It allows them a space in our awareness to be who they are. It also provides them with the wide-open possibility to discover their divine potential.

GIVING FREELY

Service is about giving without thought of return—a very important lesson. People who are mostly material-minded never really learn it. When they give, it's always as a transaction, never simply as a gift, unless it's to a member of their own family or to a friend.

Deliberate love is different from a managed heart, a phrase used to describe the way service workers, such as waitresses and salespeople, have to smile warmly at their customers, even when they're not feeling that emotion. By comparison, deliberate love is when we summon genuine love from our heart and give it willingly to another person. We decide ahead of time that this is what we are going to do, and then we do it. When we're done, we feel better. We feel the blessing of having loved.

When Jesus said not to refuse those who would borrow from us, he didn't mean that we should adopt this as a monetary policy either for ourselves or in our business dealings. He meant that unless we are capable of giving without thought of return, we haven't mastered greed.

Nothing undermines our inner peace like the feeling that others are keeping us from getting what we want. When we find ourselves in an impossible situation, where the demands on us have become overwhelming, it's our attitude toward the situation that will determine whether we will maintain our equilibrium. It is at those times that giving freely becomes our fallback position. Sometimes, it is all we can do. Rather than rail against the injustice of it all, we surrender to the demands of others and give even more than what is being asked. This is setting our ego aside for the sake of allowing the energy of the situation to move. If we resist, especially if we resist on the grounds of personal dignity, we become a block in the energy's flow. Depending on how much energy is involved, we run the risk of being obliterated by it when it finally breaks loose.

You've heard the saying, "Choose your battles wisely." The purpose here is not simply to avoid a fight but to be effective in determining its final outcome. By giving more than what is being asked of us, we become the master of the flow. We literally take control out of the hands of those in charge and use the advantage to steer events to the outcome we choose. It's a principle of judo: When your opponent lunges for you, you grab him and pull him in the direction he's moving. You help the energy go where it wants to go, adding a little extra, just to make sure it gets there.

In fly fishing, it's prudent to let your line play out when the fish is fighting against it. If you don't, the line will snap, and you will lose the fish. Teachings such as going the extra mile, giving your cloak also, and lending freely are designed to help us master our emotions—they are not meant as permanent strategies. If we have rooted out selfishness in ourselves by following these mandates, then we will be in a much better position to judge a situation on its merits and not have our thinking clouded by fear or greed. But if we are always on the lookout for unjust demands upon our time and resources, using personal pride as an excuse to hold the line, then we are doomed to eventual defeat. It is always better to live to fight another day than it is to go out in a blaze of glory. This might be a teenage boy's idea of what it means to be heroic, but it is not an effective strategy for living a successful, spiritual life.

Greed is the unwillingness to give, making it the opposite of service. It is withholding love. Unless one's heart is neutral, which is to say balanced, not biased toward giving or receiving, it will be unable to respond correctly to the demands and opportunities in life. Responding correctly is essential to effective living. Fear and desire will always cause us to respond inappropriately. And inappropriate choices cause suffering.

Consider what Irish statesman and author, Edmund Burke, had to say about civil liberty:

Men are qualified for civil liberty in exact proportion to their disposition to put moral chains upon their own appetites... in proportion as their love to justice is above their rapacity... in proportion as their soundness and sobriety of understanding is above their vanity and presumption... in proportion as they are more disposed to listen to the counsels of the wise and good, in preference to the flattery of knaves. Society cannot exist, unless a controlling power upon will and appetite be placed somewhere;

and the less of it there is within, the more there must be without. It is ordained in the eternal constitution of things, that men of intemperate minds cannot be free. Their passions forge their fetters.

The "controlling power" Burke refers to is necessary for our personal effectiveness in the world, our ability to manage our well-being and the well-being of others. It is our ability to govern *ourselves* that gives us strength, otherwise our uncontrolled passions keep us in chains. If it is empowerment that we seek, we must adopt the attitude of giving people what they need. This is service, and you cannot master it if you are reluctant to give. The practice of giving freely removes that reluctance—*forever.*

SERVICE VS. SUPERIORITY

Hierarchy breeds contempt. Jesus understood this when he said, "He who would be greatest among you, let him be servant of all." When we think we know everything there is to know about a person, we believe ourselves superior. This is the basis of hierarchy—thinking that we are on one plane speaking down to another.

The Christian custom of washing each other's feet is a recapitulation of the Middle Eastern way of welcoming an honored guest into one's home. The guest may be of higher or lower socioeconomic status, but this does not mitigate the host's responsibility to treat him with respect. Imagine what life would be like if we treated each other as though we were honored guests in each other's home.

When Jesus demonstrated this to his disciples, he wasn't saying that they were to *fix* each other. He wasn't saying that they should alter each other's feet but to *wash* each other's feet. We remove the error, not condemn the foot. This is another way of saying, "Hate the sin, not the sinner."

Washing someone's feet means that we give them, at least in that moment, a clean slate. We treat them as though they had no past. We accept them for who they are, not where they have been or what they have done. We are saying, in effect, "I absolve you of your sins." By removing the dirt from their feet, we say, "I accept you as one newly born. I extend to you the opportunity to start fresh. In my eyes, you are innocent, unless and until you prove me wrong. Even then, I will respectfully give you the benefit of the doubt."

Feet are our interface with the earth. The nerve endings in our feet connect every organ and system of our body to the ground upon which we stand—physically, spiritually (which is to say, energetically), and metaphorically. To be "grounded" means to have a solid connection with the earth—with its gravity—and to have balance in the cosmos. Therefore, washing another's feet is a way of acknowledging who they are in their totality, their wholeness. It is saying that they have as much right to be here as we do.

Treating people as though they were honored guests in our home extends also to those times when they enter our presence, our personal space. We give them our full attention. But the implication of the word "home" applies equally in this situation—*our space, our rules.* Respect is a two-way street. The less masterful the other person is in giving respect to others, the stricter our rules have to be. We do not give them the opportunity to act disrespectfully in our presence. We have to possess ourselves enough that other people will know instinctively where the lines are and that it is not okay to cross them.

With those who are proficient in the art of giving respect, the rules can relax a bit, but always there has to be a consensus as to where the boundaries are and what liberties can be taken.

Service is never an imposition upon others. Service is supporting others by giving what is needed, not by trying to change who they are. If we think we see others in their entirety, we will almost always be wrong, because only God can do that. Humans are less than perfect judges. We cannot walk another person's path—we can only help them by "washing" them of their mistaken notions. We do this by carefully and humbly attending to their needs, not by trying to change them into the people we think they should be.

Hierarchical systems go awry when they allow those who are superior, either in experience or training, to look down upon those who have yet to reach the same level of development. The whole purpose of the higher is to serve the lower —to nurture and develop, not to alter. We cannot change the other person by telling them how they should act around us, but we can show them what we are willing to accept from them, whether that person is above us or below us in the hierarchy. When they see for themselves that some things are permissible and others are not, then they have the opportunity to choose whether to adapt. This is the essence of service.

SERVING VS. CORRECTING

I am the true vine, and my Father is the husbandman. Every branch in me that beareth not fruit he taketh away: and every [branch] that beareth fruit, he purgeth it, that it may bring forth more fruit. – John 15:2

We never want to give life to the erroneous thinking of others, nor do we want to condone destructive acts. But these things cannot be forcibly removed from a person; they can only be denied legitimacy in *our* world. If the primary goal in our relationships is to be liked by others, we will be tempted to jump into their boat, to take on their state of mind in order to prove that we understand them. Instead, we should be offering them a safe harbor, a place in which they can let their feelings play themselves out and eventually return to a state of equilibrium. This is empathy, the act of acknowledging the feelings of others without feeling that way ourselves. This validates their feelings while at the same time lets us stay objective. Sympathy, on the other hand, is attuning ourselves with them, taking on their feelings as though they were our own. This only amplifies their feelings and serves no one.

Negative emotions are understandable—any of us can readily identify with another's frustration and disappointment—but we do not have to enter into that state of consciousness ourselves. It does no one any good to take on their turmoil. Instead, we say, "I understand how you feel. I've been there. Rest with me awhile, and these feelings you're having will subside. I will sit with you until they do." By doing this, we give the other person what they need, not by confronting their negativity, but by allowing them a space in which to breathe.

Unless we can maintain our own equilibrium in the face of their chaos, we cannot be of service to others. If we take on their turmoil and react to it, we only empower those feelings in the collective consciousness. We add to the negative energy instead of allowing it to dissipate. Our own peace, therefore, becomes essential to peace in the world.

Jesus uses the metaphor of the branches of a tree where the birds of the air can come to roost. The branches are the structure of our thoughts, our ideas and beliefs. According to neuroscience, this is not a metaphor but rather a literal depiction of the neural pathways in our brain. Since the ideas and the neural pathways share a common resonance, they act as receptors to ideas in the mass mind. They vibrate synchronously, just as one tuning fork can vibrate another.

It is these structures that comprise our belief system, the way we think about the world, which is hardwired into our brain tissue. It takes a lot of work to change these patterns—lots of "prayer and fasting," which is to say that we have to stop thinking along those lines, thus starving the neural pathways in question. We then begin thinking new thoughts, forming new associations that will draw new ideas to us.

The best service we can offer others is to introduce the new ideas that will start the process of reconstruction, forming new branches where different birds can come to roost. New ideas stimulate different thinking, which forms new neural pathways in our brain. The most effective ideas we can introduce are those that raise a question in the listener's mind. Questions are irresistible to the brain; it will branch and re-branch until the question is resolved. If we ask the right questions, the brain will reform itself in ways that will allow new thoughts to emerge.

The best questions are those that challenge already existing assumptions. The brain gives these questions its highest priority. It cannot ignore them. As in the example given in the beginning of this book, look at an object that your brain recognizes, such as an apple, and ask yourself, "Is this an apple?" Ask it seriously, and your brain will reboot and reconsider everything it knows about apples. As it does this, all sorts of new information about apples will flood into your consciousness.

Ordinarily, the brain runs on assumptions as a way to conserve bandwidth. Literally. The average brain has about the same amount of bandwidth as a cable modem. Thinking consumes huge amounts of calories. If the brain had to offer up everything it knows about apples every time it saw one, it would overheat. Therefore, it takes the basic sketch and then fills it in with generic details. In other words, we don't see the apple—we see the brain's combined memory of apples. But asking the question, "Is this an apple?" forces the brain to see it in present time. Then, new associations spring into being, because the present moment is always new.

(If you doubt this, I recommend that you visit the Exploratorium in San Francisco. You cannot emerge from there without your faith in your senses being totally undone. The entire place is dedicated to proving the fallibility of the human brain.)

When we challenge the assumptions other people make about themselves, we force them to look again. We raise questions in their mind about who they think they are. If we see them as inferior to ourselves, we will only cause them to react negatively, and rightfully so. No one is existentially superior to anyone else. But if we see the possibilities that are within them, even the possibility that those possibilities exist, we give them something entirely new to think about—*"Why was she looking at me like that?"* Their brain will not rest until it can come up with a plausible answer, even if it takes decades. And if the assumptions you disturb are the assumptions the other person is making about you, the same process will occur. That person will wonder why you did not play along, causing them to reevaluate their judgements of you. It will haunt them forever.

6

THE VOW OF PURITY

The troposphere is that part of the Earth's atmosphere that lies closest to the surface of the planet. It is usually about eleven miles thick, a little more at the equator and substantially less at the poles. From space, it looks like a gray haze, especially when seen from the side, due to turbulence caused by the friction between it and the ground. Air mixed with dirt, air mixed with water, air mixed with pollution—the troposphere forms a heavy blanket over everything. It is where we live.

Alchemically, air symbolizes mind, and it is remarkable how similar our minds are to the strata of air that form the Earth's atmosphere.

If we could see ourselves the way we see the Earth from space, we would see the same kind of gray haze, the same zone of turbulence, the same mixtures of different elements. Water for emotion, earth for materiality, fire for impulsiveness —all these forming our own personal atmosphere pressing down upon our awareness and creating the lens through which we perceive and interpret our world.

As with all of the five vows, the vow of purity is a tool that helps clarify our consciousness. It helps us move past the entropy of self-absorption and toward a clear vision of God. As a blessing, administered by one who has himself or herself attained the reality of clear sight, the vow of purity is a taste, a scent of the possibility of something greater than our Earthly identity, a wider and deeper reality of life that lies just beyond the boundary of self-involvement that surrounds us like a layer of fog. Once introduced to that reality, we then have something to shoot for, a ray of hope, the certain knowledge that the sun is indeed shining, in fact is *always* shining, just above the clouds.

Earth life by its very nature is a turbulent affair, and so we come to regard it as an obstacle to our peace of mind and clarity of vision. In a Buddhist analogy for meditation, the mind in its normal state of worldly involvement is seen as a pool of water that is constantly agitated by our ceaseless thinking and is therefore laden with disturbed sediment. Meditation quiets the mind, letting the suspended particles settle to the bottom, restoring the water to its pristine state. The sunlight can then pass through it unimpeded, and the mind becomes illumined.

While the turbulence of our Earthly existence seems to get in the way of our spiritual development, it is a mistake to regard it as impure. It's not that the Earth is impure, it is simply the Earth. It is what it is, neither pure nor impure, good nor bad. To shun it or, worse yet, to despise it is as misguided as despising one's own body. Nothing but suffering can come of that. But to regard the earth as the entirety of one's being is equally misguided and can cause tremendous suffering to the soul. The vow of purity is a way to see past the veil of materiality. It enables us to see the brilliant luminosity of the greater sphere of being that we also inhabit, just as surely as we do the dusty, turbulent environment of life on this planet.

Earth clings to itself. It has a kind of static electric charge, spiritually speaking, that makes everything Earthly (including Earthly thoughts) cohere into a mass of... well, dirt. Inherent within that clump, however, is the possibility for all life and self-expression. But without a connection to the clear, expansive, amniotic field of sunlight within which it exists, earth is entirely inert—no possibility for anything. In order to realize the full spectrum of life, a connection has to be made. That greater reality is the source of all power; no animation can exist without it.

Far from obliterating all things familiar, however, this pure energy brings life to what would otherwise be dead. The vow of purity is a way to harmonize one's thinking and way of being with that greater reality and thus bring about a fuller, more conscious spiritual life.

PURITY OF MIND

All of the vows point to high spiritual states of consciousness, states of mind and heart that transcend the physical body of flesh. What begins in the mind eventually works its way into the heart, and out of the heart proceeds action. When we try to bypass the heart and go straight from idea to action by way of will, darkness creeps in, and the heart recedes into the distance. This leaves a new entity, a *dweller,* parked on the boundary between our inner and outer worlds.

The dweller is the pent up energy that we are afraid to express. It looks like a devil, figuratively speaking, but it is really the life energy itself wearing a demon's mask. The mask is composed of our fears, and it mirrors those fears back to us. Depending on the strength of the life energy's head of steam—the buildup behind the mask— the evil we see there can appear huge. But it's only the mask powered by the life energy behind it. There is nothing wrong with the life energy itself. It is pure, it is good, it is holy. It is only the demon mask, a mask that we ourselves created, that makes it feel otherwise.

If we try to use our vows as a weapon against the dweller and its demon mask as a means to repress it, then we create a state of enmity between it and us. This is the worst possible use of the vows, because it puts us at enmity with our own life force. Nothing good can ever come of that. It would be better to live our life as a libertine than to be constantly at war with ourselves. No one is served when the object of life is to keep our foot on the throat of our own vitality.

Being an inner phenomenon, we mistake the dweller as our true nature—an unbridled, murderous, and rapacious lizard-self. And we resist it with our willpower. This only *seems* to work, and then only for a short while, until it bursts in upon us and eats us alive, destroying the fortress we have so carefully built to defend against it. Instead of a tree of life, our spinal cord becomes a snake, always slithering downwards, like lightning seeking the ground. But this is only because the heart has gone unattended. When our desire for knowledge supersedes our desire for feeling, when high-touch loses to high-tech, then our moral sense gets lopsided. Brute strength becomes the ideal, and our conscience is pushed into the background. Everyone loses in the end.

The vow of purity gives us the extra energy we need in order to plug into the higher strata of mind through meditation. The lower stratum is the mass mind, which is mostly concerned with life on Earth and the desires and fears that go along with it. The vow of purity helps us to identify with God's mind rather than the limited, day-to-day way of thinking that predominates in normal life. When we take the vow of purity, we formalize our intention to seek that higher consciousness. The act of seeking it draws to us the grace we need in order to realize it.

Grace is the deciding factor here. The whole idea of grace is that we don't do it ourselves—we don't attain purity by our own efforts. When we take the vow of purity, it opens a doorway, a portal into that area of the Mind of God that articulates the principle of purity. It acts upon us from the inside out. We meditate on the aspect, and then we go about our lives. The vow is like an object on the spiritual plane, a *thing* that we can hold up to the Source of all life, through which that energy will filter, shining its light upon us and lifting our consciousness high enough so that we can comprehend purity at its own level. This is what grace does.

It is by grace that the heart is awakened from its matter-induced coma and once again takes up its position alongside the rational mind as the arbiter of truth. It is the heart that moderates the power of knowledge by giving it direction and wisdom. It alone can face down the demon mask of the life force and soothe the savage beast. The pent up energy behind the demon mask is re-routed, given a higher object of desire and by degree made nobler in its pursuits.

The will we pretend to use against the demon mask is a mental construct, a mock willpower fueled only by the ego. Since the will and the life force are one and the same, force of will cannot bring about the change, because the life force cannot self-destruct. In Western mythology, dragons symbolize the demon mask. When a dragon is slain, the slayer eats its heart and drinks its blood, thus incorporating its vital energies. Only the outer form of the dragon is killed, thus releasing the vital energies it held captive.

As the grace of purity transforms us, our mind becomes clearer and our thoughts become more sharply defined. Such thoughts are powerful and have the ability to transform our lives. So, we can say that purity is the ability to think in a consistent way, to think thoughts that are unadulterated by opposing thoughts. This does not mean that we have to be closed-minded or dogmatic in our thinking. Instead, it means that we learn to use our thoughts as tools with which to fashion the outer circumstances of our lives in ways that are consistent with our ideals. It's not that we shouldn't entertain opposing viewpoints, it's that we don't, at least not when the chips are down.

When we understand the component parts of mind, we begin to see how thinking is the act of deliberately combining concepts in such a way that they attune our awareness with divine ideas. The vow of purity empowers us to see this inner dynamic of mind more easily. Once we see how the mind works, we can better use it to our advantage. Otherwise, contradictory thoughts dominate our awareness and adulterate the attunement we are trying to establish.

Divine ideas are constructs in the universal mind. Our brains tune in to them in much the same way that a radio tunes in to a radio station through a process of attunement. Concepts are the individual building blocks of ideas. For example, "good" is a concept, and so is "work" or "effort." Put the two concepts together and you have the idea that hard work will bring success.

Worthiness is also a concept. When we combine it with our self-image, then hard work tends to take a back seat, and success comes to us with little or no effort on our part. We are *lucky*.

PURITY VS. PURIST

Purity is a matter of consistency. A pure substance is one that consists of one material only, such as pure gold. An impure substance is one that has been adulterated by the addition of one or more foreign materials. It's not that one material is good and the other bad, it's that putting the two together compromises their individual integrity. It alters their individual characteristics. Depending on what you are using the material for, its purity can be very important.

At the same time, the substance of our lives is rarely pure, neither should it be. Pure gold, for instance, is impractical for use as jewelry. It's too soft. So we add other elements to it to make it harder. This is called an alloy. Similarly, the ideas that form the basis of our individualized thinking are usually mixtures of related concepts. These mixtures make our personal ideology or worldview more adaptable to our life's circumstances.

Whether better strength or a difference in color, the particular mixtures we cultivate make our individual life unique. A friend, whose mixtures are similar to ours, we call an ally, a word curiously similar to alloy.

When we understand purity in this way, we can avoid the unbalanced worldview of the purist mentality. Purists are often obsessed with their own ideas of the world and humanity's place in it. They will gladly sacrifice reason to dogma, curiosity to creed, and diversity to a monolithic sameness. The vow of purity was never intended to support such a stultifying mindset. Rather, it is a means to an end, a way to focus the mind. Purity allows the mind to play the alchemist, combining ideas in new ways so as to expand consciousness, not restrict it.

The purpose of purity is not conformity. The main goal of purity is not to conserve already existing ideas, as though healthy exploration of greater possibilities were somehow impure. Viewing it in this way only robs us of a powerful tool of mind. It is the *trajectory* of our curiosity that must remain pure. We must not seek only those ideas that will satisfy our preconceived expectations. Instead, we must be chaste to the truth, accepting whatever it may be, taking it in at whatever level we are capable of comprehending it.

Adopting another's grasp of the truth as though it were our own, without first testing it and integrating the results of our tests into the fabric of our being, is an adulteration. For no idea, no matter how true it may seem, is true *for us* if we do not arrive at it by the fruits of our own labor.

PURITY IN SPEECH

Most people think that purity of speech means no swearing. Perhaps it could mean always telling the truth, to refrain from lying. Or maybe it means to speak positively, to avoid gossip or spiteful criticism of others. Of course, purity of speech could mean any of these things, but these examples are essentially moralistic in nature, which is not the best way to access the real power of a principle. This is because morals are largely cultural and can differ widely from one group mind to another.

If we take as our primary definition of purity as "pure substance without the addition of lesser or inferior substances," then purity of speech means speaking without equivocation. Any time we add one substance to another, we obscure the original substance. We reduce its clarity. Clarity is the key word of the principle of purity. When we use obfuscation in order to hide the true meaning of our words, we violate the principle of purity in our speech.

Here again we see where purity is an aspect of humility, because in order to speak clearly, we have to tune in to the way the other person is hearing us. We have to be aware of our audience, what it is capable of understanding, and speak accordingly. We have to take our attention off of ourselves and put it on the other person. By doing this, we place more importance on their understanding than we do on our being under-stood, on communication itself rather than the satisfaction of self-expression. Our goal is to be heard rather than to simply spout off.

Pure speech also means that we strive to serve the needs of the person to whom we are speaking. We want our words to be helpful, to do no harm. If we intend our words to hurt the other person, we are mixing them with anger. Our words become a weapon and not a means of communication at all. Since the purpose of speech is communication, trying to hurt the other person with our words is to adulterate our speech, to use it for a purpose for which it was never intended. Communication is by its very nature a two-way street, a give and take of ideas and feelings. To use our speech as a weapon, thinking that we are communicating harm, is to invite retaliation, thereby negating any service to ourselves. Words spoken in anger can only lead to our own undoing.

Deception is another misuse of speech. By "misuse," I don't mean that it is speech misapplied, but that it is the attempt to use speech in a way that subverts the purpose for which it was created. Speech is the physical manifestation of the principle of communication. And since communication is the means by which ideas and feelings are shared, lying is the act of withholding. It is not sharing at all. It is offering a counterfeit in place of the genuine article, and is thus an adulteration. It is disingenuous, which means "not genuine."

The lack of clarity in speech is usually indicative of deception, as in the "fine print" of an insurance policy. Insurance companies profit immensely by dissimulation, by making their policies so hard to understand that it is nearly impossible to determine which events are covered and which are not. Such practices undermine the principle upon which the concept of insurance is founded—the shared financial risk amongst a group of people in the event of an individual's need. Dissimulation destroys trust, the very foundation of civil society. Take it away, and communication is compromised. No sane person will open up to another person if they think they are going to get hurt. We become overly guarded in our interactions, separating ourselves from our fellow human beings. This prevents cooperation, which is dependent on trust.

Of all the ways in which we can apply the principle of purity in our everyday lives, the most important is purity of speech. Why? Because purity of speech is all about telling the truth. And, as we all know from experience, telling the truth changes everything. Telling the truth is the most powerful tool we have in creating the world we live in. If we are continually trying to hide the truth from those around us—or from ourselves —we are out of accord with the principle of purity. This destroys the clarity of our thoughts and speech. To know the truth, we must be willing to speak the truth.

A word about swearing:

Rarely in every day speech does the f-word mean sexual intercourse. Normally it's used as a way to add emphasis to what we are saying. (I'm using this particular word because it epitomizes the notion of swearing or vulgar language in most cultures.) If this word was merely slang for sex, then it would not constitute impure speech. Slang is not a form of lying, nor is it intended to obscure meaning. On the contrary, we use it to improve clarity. When we properly use profanity as a tool, it can jar our listeners out of their assumptions about what we're saying and force them to re-assess our ideas. But, as a form of speech, profanity loses its effectiveness if it is overused. In this way, it can get in the way of clarity and thus become impure speech. So, we don't have to get hung up about swearing or think that if we omit swear words from our vocabulary that our speech is automatically pure. If it is purity of speech that we aspire to, then we must work on omitting equivocation, dissimulation, and all other forms of lying.

ACTION, SIMPLICITY, AND SEX

Purity of speech strives for clarity. We say what we mean, and we mean what we say. Purity of speech is being concise in our use of words. It means that we practice communication in the way it was intended—accurately conveying our ideas and feelings without contradiction and with a high degree of simplicity.

So it is with our actions. Purity of action means that we do those things that are consistent with our goals. It means refraining from acting in ways that contradict or work against what we are trying to accomplish in our life. The Transcendentalist philosopher Ralph Waldo Emerson said, "Your actions speak so loudly that I can't hear a word you say." If we fail to align our actions and our words, we are not living in accord with the principle of purity.

Simplicity is subjective. What is simple for one person may not be simple for another. We all differ in our ability to keep multiple balls in the air. As long as the overall goal of our life is consistent, then it doesn't matter how much we have going on. It only matters that one part does not subvert any of the others. If our lives become overly complicated, then it starts to show. In this way, purity equates to focus—our actions must be in integrity with our goals.

Without focus, purity cannot exist. We must be able to clear our personal energy field and decide which vibrations we will radiate. When the vibrations we emit are consistent with each other, they reinforce each other. If they are not consistent, they cancel each other out. A pure signal, therefore, is a strong signal.

Purity means one thing unadulterated by something else. But, if two things are combined for a purpose, as in the previous example of adding two metals together to form an alloy, that's different. It is possible, for example, to have pure brass, even though brass is a combination of zinc and copper. It is possible to have a democratic republic, even though one term means rule by the people and the other means government by representation. The intended use of such combinations is clear, and as long as clarity is served, there is purity.

Anytime we use words such as pure, clean, elegant, simple, or modest, the principle of purity is at work. Simple truth, elegant writing, elegant design, modest speech, a clean cut—all of these terms denote clarity and simplicity. Modesty, for example, is the opposite of showiness. Modest speech lacks excessive hyperbole. It seeks clarity and communication—it does not try to impress. In surgery, a clean cut is a precise incision, one that is in the right place and neither too big nor too small. In hunting, a precise shot makes for a clean kill, as opposed to merely wounding the animal and prolonging its suffering. In a military strike, it means little or no collateral damage.

Blessed are the pure in heart

A pure heart is a heart devoid of hatred. How do we purge our heart of hatred? By praying for our enemy's happiness. We pray for him as though we had no prior relationship with him, as though we were completely objective. This separates us from what happened—the violation or the transgression—and changes the polarity of our thoughts and feelings, thus cleansing our heart of anger and fear. When our heart is pure, we realize our oneness with the other person— we see God. As in the theme of the movie *Ender's Game*, the more you know your enemy, the more you love him.

Sexuality

Purity has little to do with sexual desire. Sex is natural and good. But, in order for it to be pure, it must be consensual. Feelings of being used can only happen when one person has different expectations about the outcome, in which case the sex could hardly be called consensual. In order for consensus to exist, there must be clear communication—no dissimulation or manipulation.

It's only when sex adulterates the other person's relationship with others, or it adulterates *your* relationship with others, that it violates the principle of purity. Chronic or habitual promiscuity is always harmful in the long run. Because of the psychic ties created in sex, multiple partners can cause confusion of one's vital energies. There are too many incoming signals, which leads to an inability to sort out one's own feelings and thoughts from those of his or her multiple partners.

Here is the main thing we should consider: sex is powerful. It creates changes in our energetic fields, the addition of vibrations that are not our own. This by itself can interfere with our clarity. Unless we are in a committed relationship with one other person—one with whom we are spiritually compatible, meaning that we harmonize energetically—we would be better off if we avoided sex altogether, if we are on the spiritual path. Once we are clear about who and what we are, then being in a committed relationship with someone of similar consciousness can be a wonderful experience and a tremendous help.

PURITY AND GENDER

It would be great if we could pluck the diamond of truth about purity right out of the ground perfectly cut and polished, but this gem is buried deep in semantic rubble. It's going to require a bit of excavating and refining before its true meaning can be revealed.

The hard fact is that the word "purity," in its spiritual connotation, has been sexualized. In its narrowest interpretation, it means *NO SEX!* But this is only because sex can make people irrational, and the authors of the no-sex rule didn't like that. Sex is disorderly and unpredictable, which makes it difficult for the thinking mind to control. And the rational mind—and those who swear by it—is all about control.

Sexual activity is fiercely regulated in all human societies. There are strict rules about how individuals should behave. After all, the physical life of the tribe depends on it, and the orderly function of its society requires strict genealogical integrity. Property rights and inheritance rights all depend on unambiguous lineages. But strangely, the rules governing such things have been made highly gender-specific. They not only define appropriate sexual behavior, they also define appropriate moral character, specifying different codes for men and women.

The principle of purity has been feminized, as though it were the exclusive province, morally speaking, of women. And the moral obligation imposed on women is severe—even an accusation of impurity can get a woman killed in some societies or, at the very least, stigmatized. Perhaps this bias towards women is due to the civic concerns listed above, those of property and inheritance. Or maybe the causes run deeper—much deeper—in the primal needs of a child for the exclusive devotion of the mother. Since most people, men especially, feel slighted from the earliest age in this department (always blame it on the mother!), keeping her affections well-regulated would seem to work to everyone's advantage, tribally speaking.

Perhaps this is why love and affection are considered primarily feminine virtues. A warm and nurturing heart is essential to child-rearing and thus essential to the survival of a people. Therefore, feminine purity is seen as the capacity to hold a space for others wherein they can grow and develop. A woman with a cold heart, however—one who has lost her capacity to empathize due to bitterness, stunted emotional development, or is simply corrupted by power—somehow loses her feminine purity and thus loses her moral legitimacy.

I could, at a point where it seems necessary to broach the subject of male purity, insert the word "oxymoron." Somehow, the words "male" and "pure" just don't fit well in the same sentence, as though they had no linguistic connection. But since warmth and affection have been commonly considered to be aspects of the heart, and since these qualities have already been exclusively reserved for women, some other heart aspect had to be claimed for men. That aspect is courage. After all, men needed some kind of outlet for their feelings that would allow them *not to be women*. The only acceptable use of the word "cry," when in the same sentence as "man," is in the words "battle cry." War, it seems (and perhaps football), is the only legitimate way for men to fully express their feelings. This is changing, of course, but all of the gains men have made in discovering their inner tender mercies could be obliterated by a single call to another world war.

Courage, therefore, is considered almost exclusively a male virtue. Men are also counted on to sacrifice themselves for the good of the tribe, but in outwardly directed ways. Courageous men are decorated as heroes. They can kill other men without letting their feelings get in the way, as long as they commit their crimes in socially sanctioned venues, such as war and criminal justice. Their ability to compartmentalize their feelings is lauded as *manly* behavior, sexualized again in the vernacular by a reference to the male genitalia. But, if a man is unable to control his emotions, it means that he is weak, or worse yet, *womanly*. The usual descriptor is wussy, or another word that rhymes with that, which further reinforces the way society genderizes moral principles. And like a woman's impurity—which is the corruption of the feminine heart aspect as it is socially understood—can get her killed, so can cowardice be grounds to execute a man, especially in times of war.

All of these conditioned ideas about purity only get in the way. They tell us little about purity as a spiritual principle. But this is nothing new. Powerful emotions have always been stigmatized in our society. And when purity is semantically linked to sex to the point where that is all that it means, people will go out of their way to get dirty.

CHASTITY AS FIDELITY

The question often comes up, what is the difference between purity and chastity? Sometimes, the two words are used interchangeably—a vow of purity is a vow of chastity, and vice versa. But there is a difference. Whereas purity is the state of unconflicted thinking—the tailoring of concepts that will best attune us with divine ideas—chastity is the commitment to keeping those ideas intact. Chastity is fidelity.

We might say that purity is a quality of thinking, and chastity is a matter of the heart. When we truly attain to the quality of chastity, we no longer want to entertain concepts that will attune us with anything less than divine ideas. Ordinary ideas that have mostly to do with mundane life become infused with higher purpose. The desire for a nice home, for example, becomes an expression of harmony and nurturance, a place in which to foster new life and to provide the substance to maintain it. But if those ideals are compromised by the desire to create an image of success and wealth, an idea composed of concepts that are ego-driven and not divine in nature, then we have chosen to be loyal to the mass mind and not the mind of God.

The vow of chastity is a kind of upgrade of the vow of purity. We commit ourselves to be loyal, to be true to God above all else, and through our commitment pours the grace that empowers us to fulfill our commitment. Chastity doesn't replace purity; it raises it to a higher level. Whereas purity brings us into the consciousness of mental clarity, chastity integrates that into our desire nature, transforming it into a one-pointed orientation toward God. In effect, we marry ourselves to God and pledge our fidelity to the divine.

Chastity does not preclude romantic love, but it does place our relationship to God above our relationship to another person. Practically speaking, our human relationships are temporary, whereas our relationship to God is eternal. Chastity does, however, form the perfect bedrock for a marriage, because if we place our own relationship to God first, we must also allow the same for our partner. The marriage vow is thus a contract for spiritual freedom, not subservience.

Chastity recognizes that God is the source of all life and power. It also recognizes that mind is a spectrum that stretches from the most mundane, animal consciousness to the most rarefied, divine consciousness. It recognizes that life is a force, an energy that pours out of the mind regardless of which part of the spectrum we plug into. The closer in attunement that mind is to the mundane, the more confused it becomes, the more contradictory the ideas are to each other, because life on Earth requires diversity. Again, one part is not better than another, only different. If our goal is to embrace a more universal and therefore harmonious experience of life, then a steadfast loyalty to the highest conception of reality becomes essential. Unless we are faithful in our striving to achieve that goal, the entropy of the mass mind will pull us down to its level every time.

There is nothing wrong with life in the world. In fact, the world runs according to the same principles as those of the vows, only in the world they are called promises. In the highest offices of government service, for instance, we promise to defend and protect the Constitution of the United States. This is a high and noble purpose...in the world. But for those who seek God, this kind of promise is insufficient. The laws of man are always subject to the laws of God. The two domains need not conflict with each other, but when they do, we look to divine principle to sort out the differences.

When it comes to God's law vs. human law, the final arbiter of truth is one's own conscience. This is the voice of God for each person, and it is *this* that the vow of chastity empowers us to hear. Individual conscience becomes the highest law of the land. This is the basis of the rights of the individual enshrined in Western culture. It is also the basis of the moral imperative of civil disobedience, when the laws of government contradict an individual's moral conscience.

In the social arena, it is the proper role of religion to help people get in touch with their conscience and to provide them with the moral support to stand by it. Ideally, the ability of a religion to provide moral leadership should be based upon the combined wisdom of the ages accepted over time by careful consideration and testing. Until we are spiritually mature enough to hear and respond to our own conscience, religion can point the way. But the goal should always be to help us develop our own moral compass, not one prescribed by others. Until we can act in accordance with our own conscience of our own free will, without having to be prompted by others, we cannot evolve spiritually. Spiritual growth can only come as a result of the choices *we* make, not the ones made for us.

Remember, the power of a vow lies in this principle: *as we move towards God, God moves towards us.* When we make the commitment to be faithful to God—to be true, as in fidelity— God is faithful to us. We get our power to live from that which we plug into, just like plugging an electrical cord into a wall socket. Taking a vow is that kind of definitive action, and the results we get are just as real.

7

THE VOW OF OBEDIENCE

It is no surprise that the vow of obedience is perhaps the most controversial of the five vows. After all, no one likes to be told what to do. Rules can be restrictive—they don't always apply to the situations in our lives. But most of all, we don't want to surrender our conscience to someone else. After all, we are the ones who will be held accountable for our actions, not them.

There is, however, a deeper, more real aspect of this vow, one that is rarely talked about,

because we don't like to admit it, not even to ourselves.

Let me explain. The typical understanding of
the vow of obedience is within the context of religious orders, which are hierarchical systems.
Brothers and sisters, whether a novice or head of
the order, are expected to obey the directives
given to them by their superiors. Organizational
integrity is necessary any time human beings
engage in a common enterprise. The more
enlightened understanding, however, is that one
takes the vow of obedience to the God Self
within, which can manifest as intuition, conscience, or impressions from your higher self.
The outer chain of command in any spiritual
group is *supposed to be* a means to get you there.
Maybe this is why Jesus said that his kingdom
was not of this world(?).

But what happens when you do get there? Are
you going to be any happier taking orders from
God than you were taking orders from other
people? I know, this a little bit like asking, "If you
win the lottery, are you going to spend the
money?" But most of us have never won the lottery, so any idea about what we would do is

strictly a daydream. The same thing is true when it comes to inner guidance.

If you believe that God loves you completely and unconditionally, taking orders might not be that big of a deal. In fact, being led in the paths of righteousness and made to lie down in green pastures actually sounds pretty good. One could do a lot worse. But the word "obedience" comes with baggage; it implies *power over*. And no one likes to have power *lorded* over them, not even (and perhaps especially) by God. As long as you see "God" as something external, perhaps the Cosmos or the Universe or anything else that is intrinsically *inescapable*, you're not going to want to subject yourself to it. Why? Because subjecting yourself to *ANYTHING* is to go against the spirit. Whose spirit? *YOUR* spirit.

If spiritual development leads to anything it leads to freedom. If it did not, the term "spiritual freedom" would be an oxymoron. And no one likes to be a moron. No one seeks mastery just so they can be mastered. If you are a saint, this line of reasoning is going to really annoy and possibly offend you to no end. Saints will vehemently protest that their relationship to God is one of love,

that their relationship to Christ is that of *bride*.
But ask anyone, even a saint, what the role of
women is in marriage, and no one, except maybe
a die-hard fundamentalist, is going to say that
women should be subservient to their husbands.

The great Geman mystic, Meister Eckhart,
said, *"God NEEDS me!"* He had a deeper understanding of our relationship to God than the
Church. The Inquisitors were going to burn him
at the stake for it, but he beat them to it by dying
of natural causes before they could bring him to
trial. Smart, that. His was a bolder, more sophisti-
cated understanding of our relationship to God.

What most of us seek is *empowerment*—the
power to live our lives more fully and authenti-
cally, knowing that such a life also empowers
others. Those who have this kind of devotion to
Life Itself see life as a dance, not a march. Their
relationship with God is a holy marriage filled
with mutual love and devotion, not as master and
slave, not even as King and subject, and certainly
not as man and subservient wife! We know that
this arrangement doesn't work in a physical marriage; why should it work in our relationship with

God? If a principle is true anywhere, it is true everywhere.

Motion and Spirit

Following the Spirit is a positive affair, because the Spirit is positive. It is always initiating action. But in order for the Spirit to move, there has to be a vacuum—a *need*. We create that need through the action of prayer. Far from begging, real prayer is setting a pattern, a *living* pattern, that the Spirit can fill. Action begets action. If we want a job, we knock on doors—we ask. If we want to be an author, we write. If we want to be loved, we find someone and love them. No intelligent person expects to move forward in life by sitting around doing nothing.

Once our living prayer has been made, it is up to us to respond to the Spirit as it starts to move in and through the pattern we have set. Once we put our *cause* into motion, we then become the *effect* of it. The movement of the Spirit sweeps through us like the wind, guiding our next move, inspiring our every thought, speaking the words we need to say in a kind of divine possession of the tongue. The Spirit ignites us with its white-hot flame, and the world responds by surren-

dering to us everything we need. And we discover
very quickly that once our life starts to heat up,
any resistance on our part—especially the resistance of doing nothing—can be hell. Once you
grab hold of the tiger's tail, you *don't* want to let
go!

Our body is set up to respond to thought, and
prayer is formulative thought. If we initiate one
thought pattern and then contradict it with
another, we add resistance to the circuit. The
contradiction will out-picture in our life. The universe, which normally comes to our aid when we
boldly commit to a course of action, will instead
present us with unsolvable problems so long as
the contradiction in our programming exists.
Obedience is a form of non-resistance to the
automatism of the unfolding of our plans.

God demands but one thing from us—that we
think and act from the deepest, most authentic
part of ourselves. Because unless we can hear our
own inner voice, how are we going to hear the
voice of God? Unless we have stripped away the
conditioning, the rules of others, the artificial
conventions superimposed on the collective
mentality of the society in which we live, how are

we going to feel the wind of the Spirit, the one that Jesus said could not be managed?

The wind blows wherever it pleases. You hear its sound, but you cannot tell where it comes from or where it is going. So it is with everyone born of the Spirit. – John 3:8

Of course, all of this can only be a recipe for disaster if one is psychopathic. This book is not for psychopaths. They don't need my help to push them over the edge. They're already there. It's too easy to slip into megalomania, thinking that everything that comes from within oneself is true.

No, this book is an update to the spiritual path —Spirituality 2.0, if you will. It's a strategy for living spiritually in the 21st Century, not the Middle Ages. Unfortunately, most of the literature in Western religion comes from that era, so we need to bring the program up to date.

Through us, as us

If you bring forth what is within you, what you bring forth will save you. If you do not bring forth what is within you, what you do not bring forth will destroy you. – The Gospel of Thomas

What is within us is not foreign to us. God
works with what is already there. Our hopes and
ideals are a living force within our heart, the inner
plan we have cultivated throughout our existence. We ignore it at our peril.

God's will for us is never a thing added from
without. The Divine continually gives life to our
own inner nature—the desire of our heart—the
same way the sun gives life to a rose. God wants
us to unfold into a fuller, more developed version
of ourselves, to be creative and inventive, to
explore the potential of our soul. What *can* arise
will arise, but only if it is already there. Why,
then, would we fear the demands of Spirit?

We must be true to that which we love. Our
heart's desire is the signature of our calling. It is
wedded to our ideals and brought to life by our
actions. When it speaks, we must listen and then
act upon what we hear. Our very life depends
upon it. It depends upon it because our heart's
desire *is* our life. It is that for which we live.

Obedience to the God Self within requires a
stepping out on our part. We must first be in
motion before we can receive guidance. And
when guidance comes, it will be creative and full

of surprises, and it will sometimes demand of us the seemingly impossible. But no one is asked to exceed their capacity, so our *yes* leads us in a journey of Self-discovery. Obedience to God, obedience to Self, inviting and then allowing God to express *through* us *as* us—this is the essence of the vow of obedience. Anything else is power over.

OBEDIENCE AND APPRENTICESHIP

It should be obvious by now that taking vows raises a person to levels of commitment significantly higher than reading books, going to church, or talking about spirituality. When you take vows in a church, it usually means that you are signing up as a deacon or some other official position. You assume some of the ministerial duties to the congregation, and you are under the direct supervision of your pastor or priest. But the point of this book is to explore the role of vows in one's everyday life in ways that go beyond a religious setting. After all, vows are deeply personal; they are a commitment to God, not to an organization.

First of all, let's look at the word "apprentice-ship" in the context in which it lives. Apprenticeship implies learning, of course, but more significantly it implies that there is a body of knowledge that already exists, and the point of apprenticeship is to learn it. Apprenticeship also implies that there is someone qualified to *teach* that body of knowledge—someone who has not only learned the knowledge itself but who has practiced it to the extent that he or she has mastered its application.

These then are the keywords when it comes to apprenticeship: mastery and application. Mastery of the ideas alone is insufficient—you can't attain spiritually by only reading books and attending lectures. In fact, too much book learning can actually prevent one from being a good apprentice, because you find yourself constantly questioning what the teacher is trying to show you. Nor can you learn from someone who hasn't lived what he or she is professing to teach, and not only lived it but lived it with some degree of success.

Let's take the example of rock climbing. Your friend comes to you and says, "Hey, let's take up rock climbing. I know this great face we can climb. It's about 100 feet high. We'll get some equipment and climb that thing!" There are two (at least) potentially fatal flaws in this line of thinking. One is that anyone can do it—anyone can climb a cliff as long as they have some equipment and the will to climb it. Secondly, there is the assumption that there is something external to be conquered—in this case, the rock . In reality, what needs to be conquered is oneself. This will become immediately obvious once you get more than ten feet off the ground. There is a lot to know before one actually attempts to climb a rock, regardless of its size. There are ropes to learn.

There is also another assumption that can lead to disaster: the notion that there is nothing really dangerous here. It just looks like a lot of fun. And, it's a cool thing to do, something that you can tell your friends about—"Hey, I'm a rock climber!" You scatter equipment all over your apartment, you keep some of it the back seat of your car, so that your friends can see it, and you wear your climbing shoes to the mountaineering store. Part of this is the getting-into-it phase of the process, but if we're honest with ourselves, we know that we're more interested in the *idea* of being a rock climber than we are in doing the work to actually *be* a rock climber.

But we're not talking about rock climbing, are we? We're talking about making a serious commitment to the spiritual path which, by the way, also has a cool-factor—"Hey, I'm a meditator! I know all this neat stuff about yoga and the kundalini, about the chakras and the Pleiades, about the Egyptian Book of the Dead and Deepak Chopra. Just check out my bookshelf." It would be far more productive, in terms of spiritual development, to spend a couple of hours a week helping out at a homeless shelter than it would be to study yet another book or spend one more minute arguing about spirituality on Facebook... eh?

These are the hard facts. The yogi Ramakrishna said, "Do not seek illumination unless you seek it as a man whose hair is on fire seeks a pond." And Jesus said, "For which of you, wanting to build a tower, doesn't sit down first and compute the cost to see if he has enough money to complete it? Otherwise, when he has laid a foundation and is not able to finish the tower, all who see it will begin to make fun of him."

Apprenticeship has a price. Make sure you are willing to pay it before you commit yourself seriously to the spiritual path.

You have probably noticed by now that I have gone out of my way to avoid the word "disciple." This is completely intentional. Why? There are two reasons. One is that the word "disciple" has too much religious baggage, most of it negative. And two, it's all too easy to equate discipleship with following a philosophy. No one would say, for instance, in today's world that they were a disciple of Ouspensky. Ouspensky is dead. Therefore, one can only be a reader of Ouspensky, not a disciple. To be a disciple of someone, you must be in their presence.

Being in the presence of someone who has mastered what you are seeking to learn has several distinct advantages. First, there are some things that cannot be put into words. They can only be transmitted. This is true regardless of what you are learning. Confidence, for instance, is not only something you develop over time as you learn a skill, it is also infectious—you can actually pick it up from your teacher. And often-times, catching it in this way gives you the neces-sary courage to try things you wouldn't ordinarily try on your own.

There is a kind of magnetic induction that occurs between teacher and student, a connec-tion that allows a transmission of real knowledge, a vibratory quality that you can take with you. This vibration disrupts the filter you already see and think through. It will poke holes in it and show you new things, new ways of perceiving the world, allowing you to respond to situations dif-ferently than you would otherwise. It does this through your intuitive and imaginative faculties, revealing itself in ways that make you think that they came from your own mind.

It is to these higher promptings that we vow our obedience, not to the demands of the teacher. Any teacher who tries to force you to obey what he says is like a gardner who tries to force his plants to grow by pulling on them. Spiri-tual growth can only happen from the inside out. The best teachers teach by suggestion and with a lot of patience, not by intimidation or threats of expulsion from the group. If you encounter such a teacher, run away fast.

We grow spiritually as a result of suggestion over a period of time. Of course, this is also how we function in the world, but usually we are unconscious of the source of our thoughts and preferences, which is the mass mind and its cultural conditioning. Usually, this kind of conditioning is for the benefit of the larger group, not necessarily for us as an individual. Our needs are subjugated to the needs of society. But the spiritual path always demands that we leave the path of others, to seek and discover our own unique relationship to the Divine. This always makes us feel like a stranger in a strange land. A legitimate teacher recognizes this and will never try to force you to do anything that violates your conscience.

Through the vibration of a good teacher, we get a higher perspective, a more universal view of the world and our place in it. We can easily identify this new vibration, because it usually wants us to step outside of our comfort zone. Life seems to get harder, more challenging. This will also change the way other people see us. We will appear out of step with the norm, and they will start to treat us as the "other," no longer a member of the tribe. This is what Jesus meant when he said, "Blessed are they who are persecuted for my name's sake…" If you're newly on the spiritual path and everyone loves you, be concerned. Unless they too are on the spiritual path, no one is going to celebrate the changes you go through.

It's this potential ostracization that makes us prone to obey the impulses of the world, no matter how strong the vibration of the teacher may be. That's the nature of being human. But as we become more conscious and make the extra effort to reach as high as we can into our intuition, it becomes easier to act on what we are hearing. And as we act upon these higher promptings, we amalgamate them, and we become transformed into a new being. The law is written in our hearts, and we no longer need to be told right from wrong. We realize Jesus' statement, "I am in the world but not of it."

THE VOW OF OBEDIENCE VS. FOLLOWING THE RULES

I live in California, possibly one of the most litigious states in the country. There is an inordinate fixation on rules out here, especially in the area of regulatory law, so much so that when it comes to environmental legislation, the rest of the states know that "as California goes, so goes the nation." Whatever is mandated here will be mandated in Peoria ten years from now. This has its upside in that one of the first things Californians notice when they travel to other states is the smell of automobile exhaust. The air quality restrictions here are so fierce that smog is almost non-existent, even on a hot summer day.

There are stark differences between the East Coast and California in the way people follow rules. Blue blood vs. Hollywood. Pin-stripes suits and wingtips vs. bluejeans and Nike running shoes. If ever there was a case where spiritual polarity mirrors geographical polarity, this is it. The East Coast has deep undercurrents of tradition, whereas in California, innovation is the norm. This may have something to do with the East Coast's colonial beginnings, the *New* England, and California's golden aura as the Land of Opportunity, the new frontier. Both reflect our own inner polarities, our Saturn and our Jupiter, our desire to be safe and our need to explore.

So it is with the vow of obedience. There are rules we must follow, and there are rules we must break. There is a natural rhythm that rules provide, a safety zone wherein we can know ourselves. But there is the unknown part that beckons, when we are ready—a calling. And it is to that calling that we owe a higher allegiance. This makes us "despised and rejected of men; a man of sorrows," as it says in Isaiah—but to our calling we must be true, even if it means that we will be alone. There is no such thing as the sound of a different drummer to those who are rule-bound.

8

PUTTING IT ALL
TOGETHER

We have to understand the importance of living a spiritual life *in the world*. After all, in the Garden of Gethsemane, Jesus said, "I pray not that thou shouldest take them out of the world, but that thou shouldest keep them from the evil." Taking vows while living a secular life affirms the goodness of life. It affirms the beauty of nature, the enormous opportunity that living on Earth is, and the unlimited possibility of divine expression that we are. Life is good; the Earth is good. Why else would the Bible say that God *so loved the world*? If God loves it, we should love it, too.

I am not denying that life on Earth is hard. It is, even in the best of conditions. Earth is a battlefield. The fight is not only with external enemies but with internal ones as well. But, if life is a battlefield, the five vows are our rules of engagement. They give us the mindset that allows grace to flow into and through us. They enable us to keep God first in everything we do. They give us the power to live in integrity with our highest spiritual aspirations.

Sometimes, the desire to live a spiritual life can lead us into false notions of piety. It is important that we identify these notions and separate them from our understanding of the five vows. More often than not, religious piety does nothing to empower those who have dedicated their life to the spiritual path, because it tends to be based upon shame and unworthiness. It tends to stifle creativity and originality. Piety becomes an external standard to which we conjure up an allegiance to a set of ideas or an organization, all in the name of being holy. But when we are honest with ourselves, we realize that we don't have a clue about what "holy" is, and we wind up aping

someone else's concept of holiness. This is disingenuous at best, and soul-murdering at its worst.

History is full of examples of men and women
who *made* history by trying out new ideas, by
taking the conventional wisdom and turning it on
its head. They did it because the current mindset
was stultifying, and the only way to break out of it
was to try something entirely new. Such pioneers
have opened the doors for thousands of their col-
leagues and breathed new life into their profes-
sions.

It's time that we update our understanding of
the five vows and use them to empower us in the
things we came here to do.

Living the Five Vows

Humility helps us to be open to new ideas, to
be innovative and creative, and to respect ourselves and others. Poverty helps us to let go of the
past, to relinquish our attachments to both material possessions and cherished opinions. Service
teaches us what real love is, takes us beyond sentimentality, and changes the polarity of our heart.
We become forces for good in the world. Purity
keeps us focused, it keeps us true to God, and
helps us see with clear vision the deepest desires

of our soul. Obedience brings us into alignment with what really matters, keeps us true to God, and opens the door to a freedom of expression beyond our wildest dreams.

Working with them

The first step is to meditate on each of the vows separately. Put yourself in a receptive frame of mind and ask God to reveal the truth of each vow to you. It's okay if nothing comes right away; sometimes the download operates strictly in the background. But fully expect lessons to pop up in your everyday life soon, even immediately. The Spirit works in marvelous ways.

When you're ready, try working with the vows two at a time. For example, take purity and service and combine them. Ask yourself this question: "Can I know everything about someone and still love them? Can I love them just as they are, or do I have to pretend not to see their dark side? Can I combine clarity and love?"

Or, try combining purity and poverty. Can you be transparent to yourself? Can you allow yourself to mourn when you let go of something you were hanging onto? Can you resist the temptation to make yourself wrong for feeling sad?

"Blessed are they who mourn, for they shall be comforted." But, they cannot be comforted if they do not allow themselves to mourn.

How about poverty and obedience? Are you able to drop what you're doing and respond to a person in need? Can you pull yourself away from a task when you realize it's a waste of time? Or, do you allow yourself to be pulled along by it, ignoring your inner guidance to move on? Who or what is your master?

Take humility and service: Can you simply answer a question without volunteering more than was asked? Can you wait for the other person to get what you're saying, or do you pre-empt the process and ruin a moment of self-discovery?

These are just a few of the ways you can turn your knowledge of the five vows into wisdom. And that's the point, isn't it? Doesn't wisdom count more than knowledge?

Wisdom is the principal thing; therefore get wisdom: and with all thy getting get understanding.
– Proverbs 4:7

ABOUT THE AUTHOR

Michael Maciel is a priest and master teacher of the Holy Order of MANS. He was ordained into the priesthood in 1972 by Dr. E. W. Blighton (Father Paul) at the Order's headquarters in San Francisco, California. In 2010, Michael was ordained into mastery by Master Timothy Harris of the Gnostic Order of Christ in San Jose, California. Since then, he has officiated and participated in priest ordinations and rites of initiation. Michael currently sits on the Board of Directors of the Holy Order of MANS, a non-profit corporation in the State of California.

You can read more of Michael's writings on the following websites:

The Mystical Christ at www. mysticalchrist.org

and *INTU* at www.intu.org

Contact Michael at michaelmaciel@mac.com or through the website The Five Vows at www.thefivevows.com.

You can friend Michael on Facebook at www.facebook.com/michael.maciel.3975 or join these groups:

The Five Vows at www.facebook.com/ groups/161829094026422/

The Mystical Christ Newsletter at www.face-book.com/groups/197925370312747/

FastPencil
http://www.fastpencil.com

CPSIA information can be obtained at www.ICGtesting.com
Printed in the USA
LVOW10s0727210615

443264LV00028B/240/P